THE
COMPANION
DOG

THE COMPANION DOG

*From Best Friend to
Obedience Ring Partner*

Glen R. Johnson

**HOWELL
BOOK HOUSE**
New York

Maxwell Macmillan Canada
Toronto

Maxwell Macmillan International
New York   Oxford   Singapore   Sydney

Howell Book House
Macmillan Publishing Company
866 Third Avenue
New York, NY 10022

Maxwell Macmillan Canada, Inc.
1200 Eglinton Avenue East
Suite 200
Don Mills, Ontario M3C 3N1

Macmillan Publishing Company is part of the Maxwell Communication Group of Companies.

Library of Congress Cataloging-in-Publication Data
Johnson, Glen R.
   The companion dog: from best friend to obedience ring partner / Glen R. Johnson.
      p.   cm.
      ISBN 0-87605-423-8
      1. Dogs—Obedience trials. 2. Dogs—Training. I. Title.
SF425.7.J64   1992   91-34549   CIP
636.7′0887—dc20

Macmillan books are available at special discounts for bulk purchases for sales promotions, premiums, fund-raising, or educational use.
For details, contact:
                Special Sales Director
                Macmillan Publishing Company
                866 Third Avenue
                New York, NY 10022

10 9 8 7 6 5 4 3 2 1

Printed in the United States of America

Contents

Acknowledgments

The illustrations in this book are expertly drawn by Sue Sellers Rose of Michigan, who is an Obedience, Tracking, and Conformation Judge. I sincerely thank Sue for her assistance and encouragement.

Many thanks also to George Baribeau, who is the Training Director of Guardian Training Academy. George picked up the lead from Glen. George absorbed everything Glen said and he remembered it. He now instructs a handler and conducts a class as if Glen were whispering in his ear.

Thanks to Sheighla Householder, who corrected Glen's grammar, spelling and punctuation when he wrote the book.

Also, I want to thank Jim and Judy Yates, who encouraged Glen to record his training methods and philosophy regarding dog training for all those handlers and their dogs who wanted Glen to write a book. Thank you to all those who wanted Glen to teach them how to train their dogs.

I want to thank Glen for writing this book. I am so glad and proud it was written before he died. Some of his knowledge and expertise has been saved forever.

For myself, I want to thank all the dog trainers who wanted Glen to write this book and Ann Pearson, whose moral support and happy dogs carried me through this time.

Sylvia Johnson

Foreword

Glen wrote this book because he felt owners wanted to be nice to their dogs, and many dog handlers were having problems with dogs either at home or in competitions. He felt that if owners trained their dogs using proper psychology a lot of problems needn't have been created.

He believed in *correcting a behavior, not a dog*. Trainers who had problems with their dogs always asked for his advice after the problem was created—not when the problem started. He hoped by writing this book he could teach handlers to avoid problems.

Also, this book is the format to higher levels of training. His training prepared dogs for advanced training from their first training session. He always taught and devised methods that would lead to more advanced training.

He believed dog owners want to own well-behaved pets, not pests. Many owners wanted written material on training a dog by his method.

He wanted all dog owners to have a well-trained dog.

S.J.

The author with one of his favorite students. *Kollander*

1

Now You Have a Dog

W HEN THE PUPPY arrives in its new home for
the very first time, the owner is faced with 1,001 questions. It is not
the purpose of this book to attempt to answer all of them. I will
assume the standard questions have been answered in one fashion or
another. You have chosen either a mixed-breed, whose parentage is
unknown, or a purebred, whose parentage is known. In either case,
you have acquired a dog: Whether a mongrel or a purebred, this
animal has now taken up residence in your home and the immense
responsibility of rearing it is yours.

Expect certain pros and cons according to its sex, some of
which can have a tremendous effect on your life. Generally speaking, the bitch has less of a tendency to want to roam, is more
protective and may be easier to train. The dog, on the other hand,
is more likely to roam *if* the opportunity presents itself, is more
bull-headed and stubborn and takes a bit more physical labor to
train. The male is the larger of the two and both usually have
acquired two-thirds of their full-grown size at six months of age.
Depending upon the breed, they might not reach maturity until

about eighteen months of age. Some breeds will mature more quickly than others and some not until four years of age.

Whatever your decision is, you now have a dog. Every behavior your dog learns from the moment it comes home is dependent upon you. Think about it: Every behavior—good or bad—is something your dog learns as the result of your actions. This makes you one heck of a dog trainer even if you don't know it! However, I would think that you would like to prevent certain behaviors from being learned and create other behaviors that will make the animal a valuable, well-respected ''pet'' rather than a pest. The process of getting your dog to that point is what this book is all about. As any person who has owned a trained dog will tell you, if they ever own another dog, and they have a choice in the matter, it will be a trained dog.

While every dog is eligible for some kind of Obedience competition, the purebred dog provides the owner with some opportunities unavailable to the mixed-breed dog. The purebred dog can be entered into licensed competitions where its performance in Obedience can be evaluated. Also, there are competitions where the animal's conformation to the breed Standard is evaluated against other dogs of the same breed. There is a distinct difference between competition in Obedience and competition in Conformation, which is essentially a beauty show. In Conformation the dog wins an award, while in Obedience the dog and handler earn awards. The mixed-breed, on the other hand, can compete in Obedience Graduations, fun matches or Correction Matches, which are held by many Obedience clubs. The mixed-breed dog requires training just as much as the purebred, and most dog Obedience classes welcome all dogs.

Dog training can be compared to a child's schooling. Children usually pass through elementary school, high school and, if they desire, college. In comparison, the dog passes from the Novice level or Companion Dog level of training (comparable to public school) to Open or Companion Dog Excellent training (comparable to high school) to Utility training (comparable to college). From this point the dog can progress to something that compares to ''postgraduate'' work, such as Tracking, Schutzhund, Hunting, etc.

Any breed of dog or mixed breed can become an Obedience trained dog.

At the Companion Dog level, your dog will learn to Heel at your side.

TWO BASIC TRAINING METHODS

There are only two methods of dog training. The first method of training is "inducive training" and the second method is "compulsive training." The difference is quite simple to understand. These terms and others are covered in chapter 13, called The Language of Training. All dog training is a form of what is called operant conditioning, not classical or Pavlovian conditioning. Most dogs that people own are physically mature animals with a few behavioral problems. That is why I will be using both compulsive training methods and some inducive methods.

This ground level obedience training course of instruction is the first step to a well-trained dog. It is designed to teach you, the handler, how to go about training your dog in basic Obedience and has been designed so that the average person can produce a trained dog after only nine weeks of physical labor, which is really the only secret to a well-trained dog.

Some of the accomplishments you can expect, provided that you put in the required time and effort described here, include a dog that:

(1) Walks at your left-hand side without pulling or interfering with your progress in any direction you may wish to go. Every time you come to a stop, your dog will automatically sit. Should you decide to change your direction or speed, your dog will always be at your left-hand side.

(2) Follows commands even when completely free of the lead.

(3) Comes directly to you when called and sits in front of you. Then, when given the command, the dog will go directly to the heel position.

(4) Goes into a standing position and stands when examined by a stranger. This is particularly useful in Conformation competition, when greeting friends or even when you want to wipe your pet's feet if they are muddy or wet.

(5) Remains in a sitting position among other people and dogs for at least one minute. Your dog will learn to lie down on

command and remain there for at least three minutes without disturbing another dog or moving out of position.

These are the rudiments of training that I will cover in great detail in this book. If you want to enter into an Obedience competition then I would strongly suggest going into an Obedience class where you will receive the appropriate types of canine distractions. Most dog training clubs or schools offer people who are training their own dogs that type of opportunity for a reasonable fee.

The methods that are described here are those same methods that have produced, for me, the first dog in history that earned every single Obedience title in all-breed competition. This included a UDTX in Canada, a UDT in the United States (there was no TDX at that time) and the European SchH III FH.

In order to make it easier to follow, I have divided the course into nine complete weeks of training that can be accelerated depending on the relative progress of your dog. The average dog or bitch requires the complete nine weeks of work. Remember, you are dealing with a member of the canine species, and they have a relatively short attention span. The dog that receives about one hour of practice each day will not learn as fast as the dog that gets two half-hour sessions per day, and that dog will learn more slowly than the dog that receives four fifteen-minute sessions per day.

A training session is just that—a working session and not a play session. Keep your training sessions of short duration, and if possible at a convenient time of the day for you. Attempt to schedule your training sessions during the same period of time every day and reserve your play sessions for the conclusion as a reward.

Do not train your dog if you are in a bad mood, and realize that alcohol and dog training do not mix. Select your training area away from home, but try to find a place as devoid of distractions as possible. You want your pet's undivided attention without distractions in the beginning.

Now, I am going to assume that you are prepared to devote one hour of your time per day in order to make your pet a trained animal regardless of its background, previous training, breed or sex. The

5

ideal age to begin formal Obedience training is about six months. However, the adage "You can't teach an old dog new tricks" is an old wives' tale and should be discarded. Any dog can learn how to acquire good habits and it is easier to avoid bad habits before they become ingrained habitual behaviors.

2

Basic Training—
Reward and
Reprimand

TO TRAIN YOUR DOG you will need two primary pieces of equipment. Like anything else, you can start out with the correct aids or incorrect aids. You will get further if you have the right equipment to begin with. You'll need a training collar and a six-foot-long training lead. Improperly used they are called a choke chain and a leash. Dog trainers refer to them as training collars and leads and employ them properly.

INSTALLING THE COLLAR

The ideal training collar is made of stainless steel and should be of a length equal to the circumference of the dog's neck, plus a distance of three inches for a small dog, three to four inches for a medium-sized dog and, at most, four to five inches for a large dog. The extra length is called the overhang. Provided it will slip over the

Training collar worn properly.

Training collar worn incorrectly.

dog's ears and has the appropriate length of "overhang," you have the correct length. The ideal size of links on the chain would be the following: Dogs weighing 10 pounds to 40 pounds should use a number two link, 40 pounds to 120 pounds, a number three link; any dog over that size, a number four link. A collar heavier than that should be used to tow cars, not train dogs. A stainless steel collar in which all the individual links are welded will start you off correctly.

There are many types of leads, ranging from the chain lead, which will probably blister and cut your hands, to the canvas type, which will result in what appears to be paper cuts on your hands. The latigo leather leads are highly favored by most dog trainers and they are resilient. They are easy on the hands and, if of the correct width, are ideally suited for dog training. The ⅝-inch width is most commonly used and is recommended for your dog training.

The six feet of length may appear at first to be an excessive length, but when properly handled it is appropriate. The same situation applies to the collar that if improperly used is called a choke chain. If it is not placed on the dog correctly, then it will not loosen and, in fact, will choke the dog at all times. If it has been placed on the dog correctly, then where the chain connects to the lead, it will pass over the *back* of the dog's neck. If it has been placed on the dog incorrectly, then the collar will pass *under* the dog's neck from where the chain connects to the lead.

HOW YOUR DOG LEARNS

Dogs learn to behave in a certain fashion because nice things happen and stop doing certain things because the niceness has been removed as a result of their behavior. Here I am speaking about the law of effect. Every action of the dog should be accompanied by an appropriate effect. I am talking about the fundamentals of learning a new behavior as compared to the elimination of any undesirable behavior. In other words:

A. Praise
B. Scold
C. Reprimand

Dogs are much like children and we have to establish certain rules regarding wanted and unwanted behaviors. In other words, normal discipline. We will tolerate certain behaviors and frown upon others. In order to establish the desirable behaviors and eliminate the others, we must learn how to administer praise properly (as well as scold or reprimand) whenever it is required so that it has meaning to the dog.

First, let me say that the actual words have no meaning at all to the dog, but the enthusiasm we say them with does. This is why I will repeat over and over again within the confines of my own dog training classes—*emote*. You can say over and over again to your dog, "You stupid mutt—how did you get me into this mess?" and depending on your mood and tone of voice at the time, your dog will either cringe or wag its tail. Let's take a look at how each of these things are performed properly.

Praise

Your dog could be the type that either reacts normally to praise or goes bonkers over praise because he or she becomes so excited when praise is administered. Because of these two different reactions, you have to be careful when administering praise. Let it suffice to say that you cannot give too much praise for something done well. However, there is a right way and a wrong way of doing it.

Praise is an example of a psychologically positive reinforcer. When you say "Good girl" or "Good boy," it appeals to the mood of belonging, which is highly pronounced in dogs. A pat is an example of a physical positive reinforcer that is administered for a desirable behavior. A dog learns to do things because nice things happen to it as a result of its actions. On the other hand, a particular behavior starts to diminish if the "niceness" is removed as a result of the dog's actions.

No dog likes to be petted on the head or shoulders so hard that the motion is jarring—that's irritating, just as it is to a human being. The correct place to pat a dog is on the rib cage behind the shoulder, or on the chest between the forelegs. If the dog is excitable, scratch it between the ears as you say "Good."

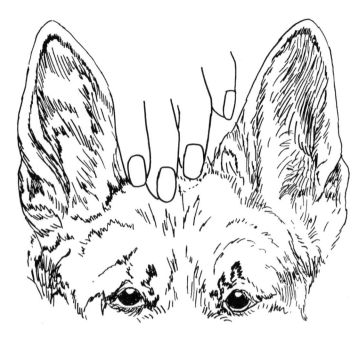

To praise, scratch your dog behind the ears as you praise verbally.

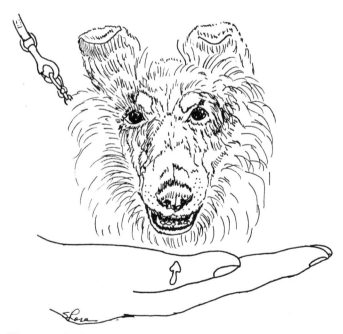

When your dog ignores a scolding, repeat the scolding while administering a quick slap to the dog's lower jaw. This is called a reprimand.

11

Scold

Whenever a scolding needs to be administered, you should select a one-syllable word that both fits comfortably on your tongue and conveys the message to "cease and desist." When either of the words "no" or "what" are delivered in such a manner, there can be no doubt that you are angry and upset. This is *not* a training type of command—after all, your dog cannot learn how to do a "no"! "No" or "what" are to be administered whenever the dog performs an action you want it to *stop*. In order to be effective, it should be given at the very moment the action you want to stop commences, not after the fact. If it becomes necessary, then set up a situation of entrapment.

Memory

When scolding, remember you are dealing with a dog. The dog's memory span is incredibly short. If you attempt to administer the scolding after the fact, then you may be scolding the dog for something other than what you want to correct. For instance, if you discover that the dog has gone to the bathroom in the house well after the act, the dog may think that the scolding is for coming to greet you. In other words, you have scolded the dog for coming to you—not for having gone to the bathroom in the house. Timing is all-important when you are attempting to train a dog.

Whatever happens, if your dog defecates in the house *do not rub its nose in it*. This is akin to attempting to toilet train a human baby by rubbing his/her nose in their own excrement. It accomplishes nothing.

If the dog has defecated in the house and you discover the crime several hours later, grit your teeth and bear it. You are too late and the only thing that would be accomplished by giving the dog hell for it might be some sense of satisfaction that you receive for having vented your own frustrations. The dog will not learn not to go in the house under those circumstances. The correct methodology for housetraining a dog is contained in the Toilet Training section of this chapter. The sooner the scolding (or the praise) is given for a particular action, the faster the lesson will be learned.

Reprimand

Quite often your dog will look at you when a scolding is given, especially if ordinary house manners are not part of its vocabulary, literally trying to "pull your chain." This is the time to impress the meaning of a scolding upon your pet, especially if the dog continues to misbehave and ignores the scolding. This is when the reprimand is applied. It is simply a means for reinforcing a scolding and is *the harshest treatment any dog needs at any time.* Any other physical abuse really has no place in training.

When your dog decides to ignore the scolding, simply use your left hand to shorten up on the lead. Do two things simultaneously. Give the scolding once more and then use your right hand with the fingers and thumb closed so as to have a closed hand to administer a sharp open-hand motion below the jaw in the fashion of an "uppercut." This should not hurt the dog, but both the scolding and the motion administered together will impress it. The scolding will now take on a meaning. In this manner the dog will discover that the same hand that brings food will also yield discipline.

Note: This reprimand is only used if your dog is lunging or snapping at people or dogs. If this reprimand does not correct the behavior, see the Problem Solving chapter and/or seek the advice of a professional training instructor or class near you.

TOILET TRAINING

Teaching any dog, especially a puppy, where to urinate and defecate can prove to be a very frustrating experience, especially for first-time dog owners. This is unfortunate because there really isn't any great secret involved. Patience and common sense, creating a schedule, coupled with a very watchful eye, is the entire key to successful housetraining in a short period of time. This applies whether you are dealing with an adult dog or a puppy.

If it is at all possible, forget paper training your puppy. It is messy and smelly, it can take a very long time to accomplish and it simply teaches a puppy that it is all right to go to the bathroom in the

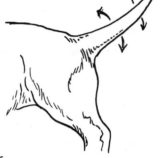

Positive

The tone of your voice and not your words will usually distinguish praise from reprimand.

negative

house. Then you'll have the problem of having to retrain. Besides, puppies really do have poor aim. Rather than putting yourself through all the trouble and exasperation of paper training, it should be preferable to prevent the dog from voiding indoors. Even as tiny puppies, dogs are clean animals by nature and attempt to void themselves in an area *other than* where they have to sleep.

Never, never punish your dog before or after Fido has committed an undesirable act. *Successful corrections are those applied during the act.* In order to housetrain the dog, simply follow these rules:

(1) Very soon after they eat—they'll have to go.
(2) Very soon after they drink—they'll have to go.
(3) When they awaken—they'll have to go.
(4) Last thing at night—they'll have to go.
(5) First thing in the morning—they'll have to go.
(6) When they suddenly sniff the floor—they have to go.
(7) Cessation of playing to wander—they have to go.
(8) Every time they have to go—get them out!

When taking the puppy out for the first time, carry the dog out. Later, escort the pup out to encourage your pet to get out under his or her own power. Watch very carefully, then if Fido makes a mistake by going on the rug (heaven forbid), it is really your mistake for not being observant enough to have recognized the mentioned signs. Scold your dog, then chase Fido out if he starts to go during the scolding process. Once outside, praise him for going in the yard.

In this fashion you have scolded him for the error *while* he was committing it and praised him for going where *you want* him to go. You have now begun to teach your dog where you want him to go. Once your puppy goes outside, in a little while he'll start looking for that same place each trip. This is why you should leave a small amount of excrement down where you want him to go, so that he will be able to locate this same spot using his sense of smell.

A night-time messer is easily cured by not feeding after 6:00 P.M. each day. If you do not leave any food or water down after this time, Fido won't have anything to eliminate after the last session outside before retiring.

As we discussed, rubbing Fido's nose in the excrement is a cruel method of teaching him nothing except fear of you. If the soiling persists, confine the dog to a small area near the foot of the bed when you retire. Being naturally clean, your dog will want to get away from his sleeping quarters to void himself, and if restrained from doing so, he will start to act up. This is your cue to get the dog outside. The longer you take to get Fido out, the greater the commotion will be, and in short order he'll be crying or barking to get out. Use common sense and don't be too slow in getting Fido out, or *you* will have made a mistake.

3

Week One— Starting Novice Obedience Training

AT THIS POINT I should mention certain crucial facts about Novice Obedience training. By following the book and completing each week of training, you will have a trained dog capable of performing the Novice or Companion Dog exercises. These exercises are listed in this chapter.

DOS AND DON'TS

(1) *Don't* practice more than five minutes or more often than five consecutive times before changing to another exercise. Because of a short childlike attention span, a dog is easily bored and will exhibit symptoms of overwork by becoming cowed or sluggish.

(2) *Do* have practice sessions not exceeding thirty minutes for any adult dog and no more than twenty minutes for a puppy less than six months of age.

(3) *Do* train often. The more often you train each day, the better trained your dog will become. Dogs (adults) should receive one hour per day of consistent work, but the training sessions should be divided as mentioned in rule two.

(4) *Don't* correct your dog until it knows what is expected from a particular command. Should it make a mistake, and it will through lack of understanding, simply start the training procedure over again. Do not use the word "no" because it is not a command, and a dog can't perform a "no."

(5) *Do* make sure you always praise when the dog performs well.

(6) *Do* end a training session with something your dog will do well. In this manner the dog will be successful and you must give a lot of praise. Your dog will remember the praise and will look forward to the next training session.

(7) *Do* spend the majority of each training session on those things with which you are experiencing difficulty. Don't avoid them—they will come back to haunt you.

(8) *Don't* spend a great deal of time on things your dog does well. They need the practice on those things that are not performed well.

THE NOVICE (COMPANION DOG) EXERCISES

After completing the nine weeks of training described in this book (sixty-three hours of work), your dog should be capable of performing the following exercises:

(1) Heeling on lead
(2) Figure-eight exercise (Basically, this is heeling.)
(3) Stand for examination
(4) Heeling off lead

(5) Recall

(6) Sit stay for one minute with you in sight

(7) Down stay for three minutes with you in sight

Once your dog is performing all of these exercises and ignoring any and all distractions, as well as other dogs in the vicinity, your pet can be classified as a *trained dog*.

THE BEGINNING—FROM FOOTWEAR TO FOOTWORK

(1) Clothing and footwear

(2) Training locations

(3) Holding the lead

(4) Correct position of the dog for Heeling

(5) The jerk

(6) Heeling on lead

(7) Sitting while in motion: the Halt

CLOTHING AND FOOTWEAR

When you are training your dog, dress accordingly. Because it involves a great deal of movement, including turns and changes in speed on your part as well as the dog's, wear comfortable clothing. More important, invest in a pair of running shoes that will give you a good grip on the walking surface where you are training. Wear the same type of clothing you would wear to clean the garage. It is not unheard of to experience a minor fall when training and grass can stain badly. Don't wear dresses or suits. Jeans are most commonly worn. Dog training is hard physical labor and there are no magic buttons you can press to have the work done for you.

Flea collars or leather collars worn with the training collar are counterproductive, as are identification tags, etc. (Put the flea collar into your pocket and you will resolve any and ALL of your flea problems.) Remove any ID tags on the dog's collar, including li-

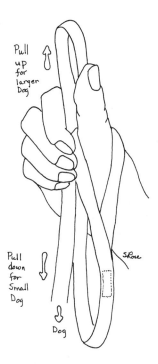

Pull
up
for
larger
Dog

Pull
down
for
Small
Dog

SRose

Dog

Lengthen or shorten the lead by
changing the length held in your
right hand.

SRose

Leads held correctly.

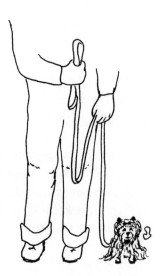

censes, etc., because these tend to telegraph every move that you make. Put them onto a snap that you can remove when training and replace them when not in an actual training session. You should not have your dog wear the chain training collar when you are not training, for these can create all kinds of physical problems for your dog. When your dog is in a training session, have your pet wear a leather or canvas collar that contains all of this paraphernalia.

Training Locations

Do not train your dog in your own yard. Princess looks upon home much the same as we humans do. We don't like to have to work when we come home—neither will she. Home is a refuge, a place to relax and to do what we want to do. Keep it that way for your dog as well.

Instead, select a place away from home even if it is only one block away from home. Better still, a school yard after school is out, a church yard or an area in a shopping plaza away from the crowds. Select a quiet place *away* from home that is relatively free of distractions, for you will want your dog's undivided attention when attempting to train. Distractions will be employed intentionally at a later stage of training.

Be well advised that in the beginning *only one* person does *all* the training. After the training has been completed, then you can instruct another member of the family as to what they have to do in order to achieve the same results. Once trained, your dog should work for another member of the family with no problem. After about seven weeks of training, you can practice your dog at home— after the responses have been learned by your dog.

Holding the Lead

To hold the lead properly:

(1) Place the loop of the lead over the thumb of your right hand.
(2) Hold up the right hand as if you were asking a question in school.

21

(3) Simultaneously, while holding the lead with your left hand at about the midpoint, move your left hand up and your right hand down until the left hand is higher than the right hand.

(4) When your left hand is higher than your right hand, reach in toward the lead with your right hand. Grasp both vertical portions of the lead with your right hand at about the midpoint, making a figure eight out of the lead.

(5) Ensure that your right hand grasps all the lead at the middle of the figure eight.

(6) Now, release the lead from your left hand.

(7) The lead should pass from your right hand down below your left knee and up to where it connects onto the collar, provided that the collar is the correct length.

(8) The lead can be either lengthened or shortened simply by adjusting the length held in the right hand.

When your dog is sitting at your left-hand side facing the same way you are facing, grasp the lead as if you were going to shake hands with your *left* hand (your thumb should point up). Move your left hand down the lead about a foot away from the chain with the thumb still pointing up. Lower your right hand until you can place it against your stomach. There should be sufficient length for the lead to pass below your left knee and come up to where it connects to the collar. If not, adjust the length until this has been accomplished.

Correct Position of the Dog for Heeling

Now the collar and lead are correctly installed and you are ready for your first lesson in teaching the dog to walk at your left side. This is called Heeling.

Before commencing, make sure that you have an appreciation and understanding of what an appropriate and correct heeling position is. If the dog is in a position of being too far behind you, it is called Lagging, while a position too far ahead of you is called Forging. To give you an understanding of the distance between you

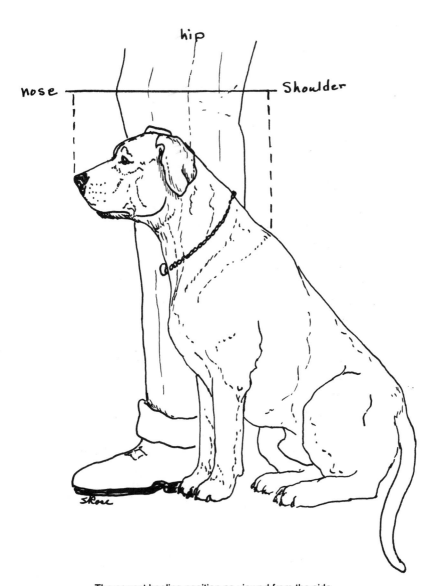

The correct heeling position as viewed from the side.

Lagging. The dog is too far behind the handler.

Forging. The dog is too far ahead of the handler.

and your dog while you are heeling, you should be able to touch your dog with the area between the thumb and forefinger of your left hand when the fingers are extended but held close together. This allows the dog to range a distance of only about six inches away from you.

When your dog is at your left-hand side, whether Heeling or Sitting, Fido should be close enough for you to touch him with your forefinger while touching yourself with your thumb.

Ideally when the dog is beside you, the dog's ears should be even with your left knee. There should be no daylight between a dog's nose and your left leg, or it is Lagging. A dog's front feet should never be ahead of your feet, or it is Forging. The only trick to teaching your dog to Heel properly is in maintaining this perspective, no matter what direction you head or how fast you go.

The Jerk

Most of dog training involving movement of any kind requires you to know how to administer what is called a jerk on the lead. Jokes have been made wherein dog training is directly proportional to the jerk at the end of the lead! Unfortunately, this is easy to say but difficult to master properly.

A jerk on the lead occurs when the lead *momentarily* becomes tight and is immediately followed by slackness. You really cannot apply a jerk if the lead is already taut. The dog doesn't make the lead go tight—the handler does. If the handler wasn't on one end of the lead it would be slack all the time.

Envision the trick performed in the dining room when the table has been set with dishes, glasses and food. The magician takes one end of the tablecloth, and with one deft snap (jerk) removes the tablecloth without disturbing a single dish or glass.

A jerk on the lead is performed in a similar fashion. If necessary, you may have to give the dog a little slack and then administer the sharp, popping jerk, immediately allowing the lead to become slack.

Remember—*it is far more cruel to tow your dog around than it is to administer a sharp jerk on the lead.* Towing your dog is akin

While heeling, the proper distance between you and your dog is approximately six inches.

1)

Slack

2)

JERK

3)

Slacken again

The jerk.

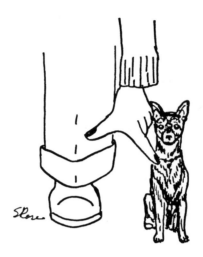

If you can touch your dog with your forefinger, and yourself with your thumb, your dog is close enough to you.

or

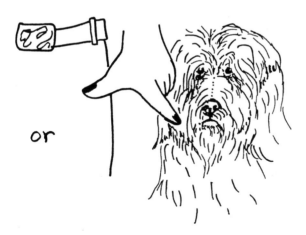

to strangulation, and is partly why the collar has the misnomer of being called a choke chain.

Heeling on Lead

This exercise and the subsequent exercises during the first week of training should be performed away from the home and play areas. The training area selected should be quiet and relatively free from distractions so that you will have the dog's undivided attention. When you walk forward, you want your dog to stay at your left side at all times. Before starting, get the sequence of events down pat. They are as follows:

(1) Use the dog's name. This is to get the dog's attention so that Princess is aware that something is about to happen.
(2) Give your dog the command to Heel.
(3) Step forward with your right foot.
(4) Simultaneously apply a sudden, sharp jerk, as described previously, *parallel* to the ground and in the same direction you are heading.
(5) Talk to your dog all the time. It really doesn't matter what you say as long as you say it with *excessive enthusiasm*. This talk can be silly talk as long as it obtains and retains your dog's attention.

Most dog training, in a class setting or in other books, states that you step off with your *left* foot. I believe that procedure must stem from the military. Here, they march by the command "By the left quick march." I cannot understand this phenomenon because it violates the most fundamental law of physics when dog training.

By starting off on your right foot and at the same time applying the sudden, sharp jerk with your left hand, the movement of the jerk is in the same direction as the right foot. This permits you to administer the most powerful and sharp jerk because the motion with the left arm balances the movement of your right foot. It is also easier to walk when the left hand moves in the same direction as the right foot—if you doubt me, try and walk with your left hand moving forward while the left foot moves forward.

To administer the jerk while stepping off on the left foot would be awkward to say the least, and later you could end up "kneeing" your dog. By stepping off on the right foot you permit your dog time to get off its rear before the movement in a forward direction has really started. Later in your training, starting off with the right foot will have a definite advantage, especially when performing the figure eight, or in competition should your dog sit with its front angled across the front of you.

Once you are moving, the lead *must* remain slack at all times or else you won't be able to administer another sharp jerk should it be required. Anytime you give your dog a jerk, it should *always* be in a direction *opposite* to the dog's intention. Especially if the dog's direction is opposed to yours. In other words:

- If your dog starts to forge ahead, you administer the jerk back.
- If your dog starts to get too far away from you, administer the jerk toward you.
- If your dog slows down and begins to lag or is distracted by something behind it, the jerk should be in the direction you are heading.

If the reason for the dog's lagging is because it is uncertain or scared, then no jerk should be applied. Instead, the dog needs your enthusiasm and encouragement. Here is where the loud, silly talk really comes into play.

Every time your dog gets out of a "good heeling" position, the jerk should be applied. What you are doing is simply taking the niceness out of being anywhere except in the appropriate heeling position, and once there, all kinds of nice things can happen.

When your dog is in the correct position—*praise* your dog lavishly, and with your left hand, pat Princess on the rib cage or scratch her between the ears. In this manner the dog has a choice to make: to remain beside you where nice things happen—or out of position, which becomes uncomfortable, especially when that jerk is applied.

At this stage of training your dog really has no choice because you are going to physically insist that she go with you. If Princess

When coming to a halt, transfer the lead to the right hand.

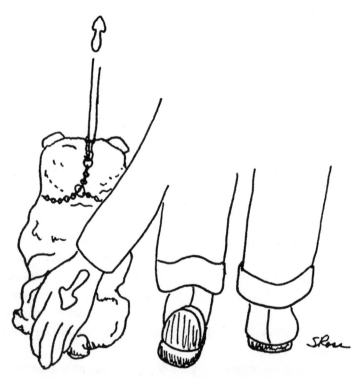

With the lead in your right hand and your dog in the heel position, simultaneously say "Sit," bring your left foot up to the right, jerk the lead up with your right hand, and with your left hand, press the dog's hindquarters to a sit position.

doesn't want to move with you on her feet, then let her try her backside. It won't take very long before your dog discovers that it is easier and more comfortable to walk on feet and move with you willingly!

SITTING WHILE IN MOTION: THE HALT

When coming to a stop (Halt), you should carry out the following sequence of events:

(1) Take the portion of the lead from your left hand and grasp it all in the right hand. You should now be holding the lead in the right hand below the point where the left hand was holding it.
(2) While still moving with your dog in the Heel position, and with all the lead grasped in the right hand, you perform steps three through six simultaneously—
(3) Command your dog to sit,
(4) Bring your left foot up to the right,
(5) Jerk *straight* up with your right hand and
(6) Press down with your flattened left hand on the dog's rump.

In this manner you are treating your dog like a teeter-totter. The front end goes up at the same time the rear end goes down. The praise *must* be given the moment your dog sits.

Great care must be taken *not* to get into the habit of stopping and *then* attempting to force the dog's rear down. If you do so, the dog can brace its hind legs and you will encounter a "battle royal." Even a small dog can brace itself to support a full-grown adult on its hindquarters! In order to be completely successful at getting your dog to sit beside you every time that you come to a halt, you must simultaneously jerk the lead up with the right hand and press down on the rump as your left foot comes up beside the right.

There is a space or indentation just in front of the dog's hind leg similar to a "pocket." It is tempting to reach over with one's left hand to slide the dog toward oneself by pulling on this "pocket," especially if the dog sits out away from you. *Don't do it!* At this point in the dog's anatomy there is a long muscle stretched over the kidney, and pressure exerted on this area is very painful. It may seem tempting at times, but don't do it. In short order, you'll have your dog swinging away from your side to avoid the pain it will come to expect every time you attempt to halt.

4

Week Two—
Changing Direction

---

(1) The stationary right turn
(2) The about turn (in motion while heeling)
(3) The right turn (in motion)
(4) The left turn (in motion)
(5) The circle right
(6) Changes in pace (fast—slow)
(7) The Stay

THE STATIONARY RIGHT TURN

First, I will attempt to give you a bit of insight concerning how the turns are made. This information will come in handy when you are trying to execute any of the turns.

All of the turns are made by pivoting on the ball of your left foot, regardless of the direction you wish to turn: right, left, about or circle right.

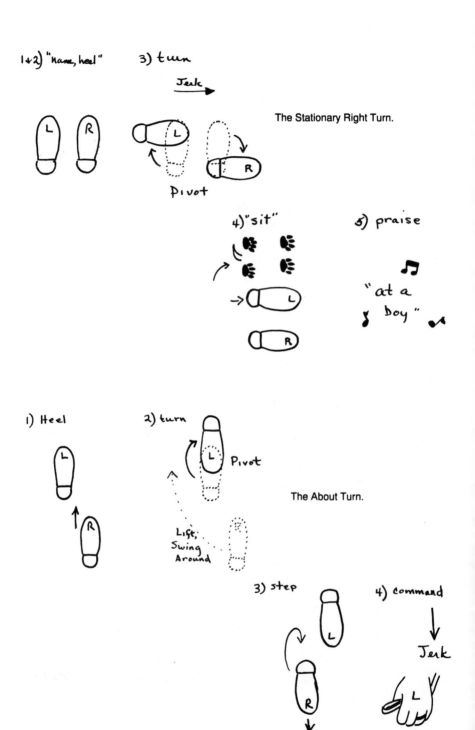

1+2) "name, heel"   3) turn

Jerk →

The Stationary Right Turn.

Pivot

4) "sit"   5) praise

"at a boy"

1) Heel   2) turn

Pivot

The About Turn.

Lift, Swing Around

3) step   4) command

Jerk

34

First, ensure that your dog is sitting properly at your left side in the correct heeling position. Then, follow this sequence of events:

(1) Use the dog's name (to get your pet's attention).

(2) Give your dog the command to Heel.

(3) Pivot on the ball of your left foot and with your *right* foot take a short step to your right, simultaneously applying a sharp, popping jerk parallel to the ground in the direction you are heading.

(4) As you bring your left foot up to a point even with your right foot, give your dog the command to Sit, and change the lead in the right hand in preparation to make your dog sit as has been described.

(5) The moment your dog sits, praise it effusively.

THE ABOUT TURN (IN MOTION WHILE HEELING)

As all of the turns are made by pivoting on the ball of the left foot, you can mentally prepare yourself for this one before its execution. While Heeling with your dog, anticipate making a turn and then follow this procedure:

(1) Stop on your left foot, pivot 180 degrees and give your dog the command to Heel. Do not use the dog's name.

(2) Turn completely in the new direction.

(3) With your right foot, begin to move in the new direction.

(4) Administer a sharp jerk in the new direction of travel *after having made the turn.*

(5) Proceed to walk at a normal speed in the new direction.

THE RIGHT TURN (IN MOTION)

To make a right turn while in motion, simply do the following:

(1) Take note of where it is that you want to make the right turn before you get there. Once there, pivot on the ball of your left foot.

(2) Give your dog the command to Heel.

(3) With your right foot, step off in the new direction.

(4) Administer a sharp jerk, parallel to the ground in the new direction. Follow the movement with a great deal of enthusiastic silly talk and praise.

THE LEFT TURN (IN MOTION)

There are two different ways of executing the left turn because of differences between dogs. Essentially you have the kind of dog that is beside the handler, or like most dogs, a little ahead of the owner. This type of dog makes turning difficult. Here the problem is getting the dog out of the way *without* having to resort to kneeing the dog when it interferes. In any case, the interfering dog is handled in this manner:

(1) When heeling, if your dog is a small distance in front of you, pivot on the ball of your left foot and command your dog to Heel.

(2) Use a sharp jerk *backward*. By using this jerk backward you can maneuver your dog away from being in front of you the moment before you execute the turn.

(3) Swing your right leg in front of the dog while pivoting on the ball of your left foot.

(4) Command your dog to Heel a second time.

(5) Use a sharp jerk parallel to the ground in the new direction of travel.

The second type of dog is *not* forging ahead of you when you want to make the left turn. In this case, you can eliminate the first jerk backward. This jerk backward is only used if the dog is, in fact, forging when you are about to make the left turn.

THE CIRCLE RIGHT

The circle right is a 360-degree turn on the spot while heeling with your dog, either on or off the lead. Problems can occur if your

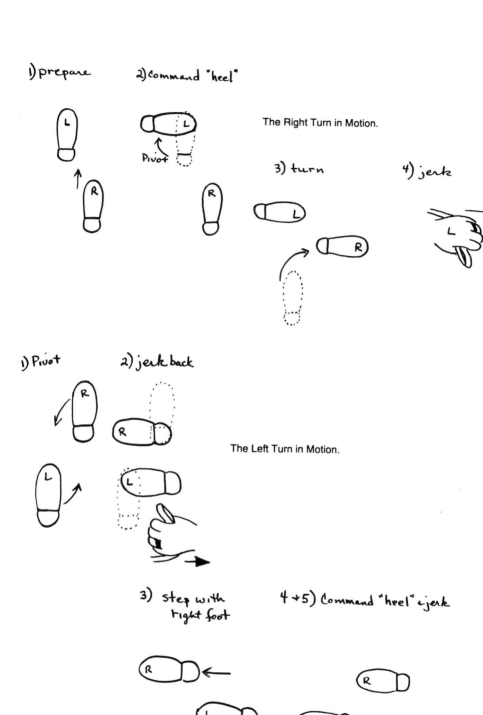

1) prepare 2) command "heel"

The Right Turn in Motion.

3) turn 4) jerk

Pivot

L

R

R

L

R

L

R

L

1) Pivot 2) jerk back

The Left Turn in Motion.

R

R

L

L

3) step with
   right foot

4 +5) Command "heel" + jerk

R

L

R

L

L

dog isn't taught how to make a circle right. Here is how you train your dog to perform the circle right when in motion:

(1) While heeling at any speed with your dog, pivot on the ball of your left foot.
(2) Execute three turns on the spot, each one a little more than 90 degrees each time.
(3) Upon completion of this maneuver, you should be heading in your original direction.
(4) There is a strong possibility your dog may become confused during the initial attempt of this unusual maneuver, so be sure to really praise it upon a successful completion.

CHANGE IN PACE (FAST—SLOW)

The normal speed is a pace you should maintain at all times. In other words, a brisk walking speed while you are talking jovially to your dog all the time. Whenever you want to change your speed, do not give a command. Instead, phase into the change of speed and accompany the change in speed with a corresponding sharp jerk in the direction of the speed change. If the pace slows, use a jerk backward, and if it becomes faster you would apply a jerk in the forward direction.

The normal speed, walking speed, when you are training a dog to Heel corresponds to a situation in which you are late for an important appointment. *Slow*: Walking literally heel-to-toe. *Fast*: a jog, or a slow run. This is the normal speed of walking when you are training your dog to Heel. When you want to change speed from a slow walking speed or a fast speed, always precede your change in pace with a command to Heel and a short popping jerk in the direction of the speed change.

THE STAY (SIT STAY)

This exercise is one of the more important tasks your dog will have to learn, as many other exercises depend upon learning it properly. Realize that from the beginning your dog is not likely to know what the command means. Because of this lack of knowledge, you really shouldn't give your dog a correction for not performing properly before the command has been learned. Let the dog *learn* the meaning of the command first before you "get tough." Initially, arrange the exercise so that the dog cannot make a mistake. If the dog does break a Stay command, simply start all over again. At the same time keep repeating the command like a broken record. To teach your dog the Stay command, do the following:

(1) Place *all* of the lead from the right hand into the left hand.
(2) Do not use your dog's name.
(3) Raise your right hand (flat, palm opened) and give the dog the hand signal to Stay as you command the dog to Stay by passing the right hand directly in front of the dog's nose.
(4) Do not touch your dog at any time. Simply pass your hand in front of the dog's nose. Continue to remind your dog to Stay.
(5) Swing your left foot immediately in front of your dog, pivoting to stand before him so that Fido ends up with his nose directly in front of your knees.
(6) Start with a ten-second wait.
(7) Remind your dog to Stay, then retrace your steps back to the right side of your dog.
(8) Praise your dog enthusiastically, and each time the dog is successful, increase the time of the Stay exercise.
(9) During this week increase the distance between you and your dog during the exercise by first reminding him to Stay as you take another step back. By the end of the week, your dog should Stay for one minute while you are standing at the end of the outstretched lead.

This concludes the second lesson of training.

At this early stage of training select a place that is without distractions and one where the dog is not allowed to play. It is of utmost importance that you have your dog's undivided attention. Do not allow play sessions until after the training sessions are over.

During the first week of training, you will have spent seven hours of training (six if you want a day off). This week will take you an additional seven hours (six) of work during which time you have all of the first week's material to practice as well.

When practicing this week's lesson, allow your dog to select both the direction and speed, then demand that Fido do the *opposite*. Insist that your dog conform to your command—not you to his. *It is amazing how many dogs make better people trainers than people make dog trainers.* Don't fall into this trap!

5

Week Three— Separating Dog and Handler

(1) No (chastisement)
(2) Leave your dog and go to the end of the lead
(3) Step back and call your dog
(4) The Stand
(5) Obstacle heeling
(6) The Down (from the side)

Up until now, you have been taught the jerk, how to get your dog started in heeling, changes in pace and several turns. The turns in motion were as follows: the about turn, the right turn, the left turn and the circle right. By now you have had the opportunity to work your dog for fourteen hours, and you should be able to see some initial progress. Now I will commence the third lesson, in other words, the third week of hard work.

NO (CHASTISEMENT)

By now your dog is starting to understand the meaning of the command to Stay. It is time to combine two words together: the command "Stay" and the word "no." You must let your dog know that you become upset every time the command to Stay is not heeded. This is accomplished by letting your dog know in no uncertain terms that you are upset when the Stay command is broken. This is accomplished by putting to use the cease and desist order, "no," at the very moment your dog breaks the Stay position. Timing is all-important if you want it to become effective. This means that you must become observant of your dog's behavior whenever you begin to depart. The very moment that the dog begins to break position, say no, then return and place the dog back in the original position.

Note: Never, never leave your dog in bad graces. Praise the dog for simply having resumed the position that was broken and start again. You will have the opportunity to do this during the next exercise.

LEAVE YOUR DOG AND GO TO THE END OF THE LEAD

(1) Place your dog into a sitting position beside you.
(2) Put the loop and all the lead in your left hand. (This will free your right hand.)
(3) Let all the lead fall to the ground except for the loop you are holding in your left hand.
(4) Use your right hand to signal your dog to Stay, and simultaneously—
(5) Give your dog the command to Stay.
(6) While observing your dog (using your peripheral vision), step off with your left foot and walk at a normal speed directly away from your dog. You want your dog to realize that when you step off on the right foot, you want the dog to Heel, but when you step off with the left foot, it is a Stay command. In other words, your right foot is your heeling foot, and your left foot is your Stay foot.
(7) The moment your dog *begins* to move out of position, chastise with a sharp *no*, immediately return to Princess and start the exercise over again.

" STAY "

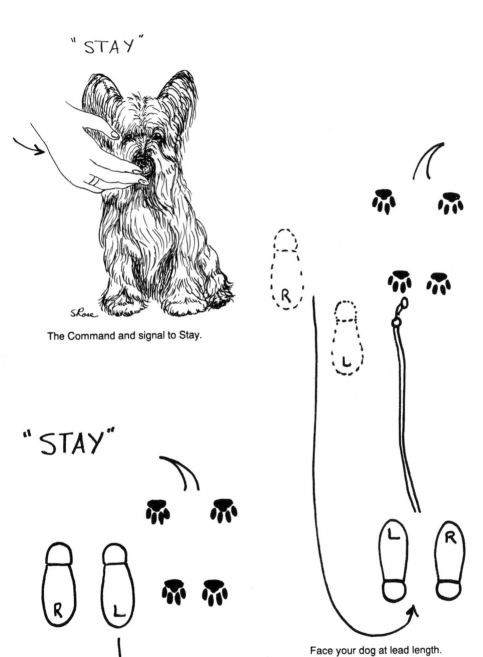

The Command and signal to Stay.

" STAY "

Leaving with the left foot.

Face your dog at lead length.

(8) Don't forget to praise her for sitting. Then leave your dog again.

(9) Constantly remind Princess to Stay as you gradually build up the time. Increase the time until she is Staying for at least two minutes before you step back to her side by retracing your steps.

As I have already stated, *don't* leave your dog in bad graces. She cannot understand this kind of behavior as we humans can. Continue to remind your dog to Stay—it doesn't cost you anything and you want your dog to understand the meaning of the Stay command. Remove the niceness by saying the word "no" if she breaks the Stay command. You certainly *do not* have to reprimand her for breaking.

STEP BACK AND CALL YOUR DOG

Whenever you attempt to teach your dog to come to you when it is called, several exercises are involved. They are taught in a certain order so that they can be understood by the dog. It is easiest to begin to teach this exercise from the sitting position while the dog is close to you so that you can enforce and control it. This is the first exercise that leads into the formal Recall so that when you call your dog it will come directly to you and sit in front of you.

In order to begin teaching this exercise, simply do the following:

(1) Sit your dog at your left-hand side in the Heel position.

(2) Take all of the lead into your right hand close to the snap (about six inches away).

(3) Use your dog's name to get its attention.

(4) Step directly backward, starting with your right foot. Do not turn in any direction. Take one or two steps backward for small dogs, two to three steps for medium-sized dogs and three or four steps for big dogs. Simultaneously administer a sharp jerk in the backward direction you are moving and command your dog to Come.

44

(5) As your dog turns to face you, reach over its back with your left hand.

(6) Stop your backward movement, simultaneously give the command to Sit, press down with your left hand on the dog's rump and jerk up with your right hand.

(7) Remind your dog to Stay, then step to the side.

(8) Praise profusely.

The purpose of this exercise is to get your dog to face you and to start heading toward you whenever the dog's name is given with the command "Come." This first exercise leads into several others that finally culminate in the entire Recall.

Dogs, as a rule, are not stupid creatures. Over the years, whenever their owners wanted to give them a reprimand or a punishment, the owner who discerned misbehavior on the dog's part usually called the dog to come and then proceeded to give the reprimand. Quite rapidly the dog learned to interpret what the command "Come" really meant—"Head for the hills, I am in trouble." As a result, the dog learned to run away whenever the owner called. In other words, the dog was punished for coming when called, *not* for any indiscretion.

If your dog has performed a misdeed, regardless of what it might be and as hard as it might be to do, handle it in the manner of the following example: If your dog has chased the neighbor's cat and you have called Fido to come back to you, which he does, grit your teeth, bear it and praise the dog for coming back to you. If you want to spank your dog for something he is doing now, then you should head toward your dog and correct him when you get to him. Never have your dog learn that the command "Come" means that he is in trouble.

THE STAND

After your dog has been playing in the rain or mud and you want to let Fido into the house, it is nice to be able to command your dog to Stand and have him remain Standing while you wipe his feet

Initiating the command to Come. Step back with your right foot as you give a quick jerk with the lead and say "Come."

After stepping back, the dog will be facing you.

46

before he is allowed into the house. It helps preserve your floors and your good nature. To teach the Stand, there are three distinct maneuvers:

(1) While you are Heeling with your dog, place all the lead from your right hand into your left hand and keep on moving.

(2) While moving, step in front of your dog with your right foot and continue to move backward.

(3) Reach down with your right hand. With your fingers and thumb close together, point your hand at your dog's chest and keep on moving backward.

(4) Use the command "Stand." As you come to a stop, reach down with your right hand, allowing your dog to run into the open right hand. Use this hand to check your dog's forward motion.

(5) Always keep a slack lead when doing this exercise, and don't ever allow the lead to tighten up.

(6) Every time your dog attempts to sit, take one step back and give the command "Stand" even if you have to take many single steps back. If you cannot get the dog to Stand with this method, refer to the Problem Solving chapter of this book for further advice.

(7) With your right hand (which has stopped your dog's forward motion), simply scratch your dog on the chest until he has settled down, and then give the command "Stay" while you stand up in front of the dog.

(8) Increase the time until Fido is standing for a period of one minute in front of you, and then remind him to stay while you take one step back. Continue doing this until you are back at the end of the lead.

OBSTACLE HEELING

In this exercise allow your dog the opportunity to get into trouble and work it out alone. It will make your dog's Heel more

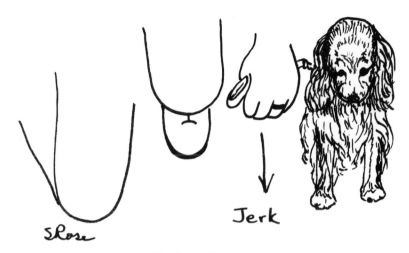

Jerk

The Down with pressure.

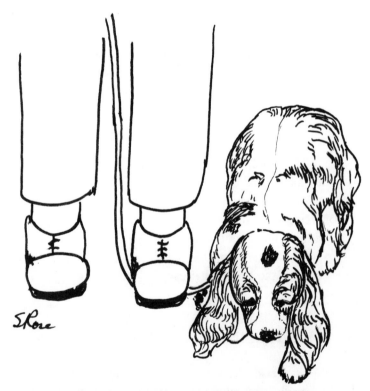

Assuring the Down position with the lead under your foot.

closed and cause it to become more observant of where you are going. This exercise is performed in the following manner:

(1) While Heeling with your dog, head toward the left of an obstacle such as a parking meter, a telephone pole or streetlight.
(2) Do not use any command, but very suddenly move to your right around the obstacle and permit your dog to tangle the lead around the obstacle.
(3) When the lead becomes tight, wait until your dog figures out how to get around the obstacle without endangering itself. In this fashion it will learn to Heel more closely, and to watch for obstacles like this.

THE DOWN (FROM THE SIDE)

At this stage of training your dog should be a little tired, which makes this next exercise easier for you to complete. You are going to teach your dog to lie down on command. Some dogs do not like being down, especially if there is another dog nearby. This is a position of submission and one from which a dog cannot defend itself. Your dog may fight the act of being down on command, but it is a battle you must win. Hopefully you will master this situation the first time. In order to perform this exercise, do the following:

(1) Make your dog sit at your left-hand side as if you are going to Heel.
(2) Place all of your lead into your left hand so that you are holding it close to, but *not on*, the snap.
(3) Do *not* use your dog's name. Raise your right hand and arm as if to ask a question and give the command "Down."
(4) Step back on your right foot and drop to your right knee.
(5) Bring your right hand down to grasp the lead close to the snap.
(6) Apply one sharp jerk downward and then use constant pressure downward until your dog is lying down.

(7) Pass the lead under the ball of your left foot and reassure your dog, letting it know there is nothing to worry about. If you want to, give your dog a tidbit for being down.

(8) Command your dog to stay, then you stand up alongside.

You are starting into your third week of training. Once you have completed this week of practice, you will have accomplished twenty-one hours of training and the progress should be noticeable. When practicing, continue to use the same type of area with no distractions, and practice should total about an hour per day. Now you are ready to start the fourth training lesson.

6

Week Four— Moving On: More Exercises

---

(1) Return around your dog
(2) Extending the Stay distance
(3) The Finish
(4) The Stand
(5) Back up and call your dog
(6) Wagging its tail

RETURN AROUND YOUR DOG

Up to now you have always retraced your steps to get back to the left side of your dog during the exercise "Leave your dog and go to the end of the lead." Now the route back to its side is going to change. In order to properly execute this exercise, do the following:

(1) When you are *away* from your dog at the end of the lead, you will be ready to start this exercise. Place the loop of the lead in your right hand.

(2) Remind your dog to Stay, then reach out in front of you with your left hand.

(3) Grasp the lead at about midpoint between the thumb and forefinger of your left hand.

(4) Start walking toward your dog's left side.

(5) Walk at a normal speed completely around your dog until you are back in the heeling position.

(6) Hold the lead at about the midpoint with your left hand so that the snap doesn't move. With the left hand holding onto the lead, prevent the lead from flapping on your dog's muzzle.

EXTENDING THE STAY DISTANCE

The Stay is practiced in all positions: Sitting, Down and Standing. The Standing position is *not* included in the extension of distance. To extend the distance I am going to assume that when you are standing at the end of the lead, your dog is able to remain sitting for at least two minutes, and in the Down position for at least five minutes. Always remember that it is more important to have your dog Stay for a long time with you up close than to Stay for a short time at a long distance. In other words, time is more important than distance. When you are up close, you can correct your dog much more quickly in case of a break. To extend the distance correctly, do the following:

(1) Leave your dog and go to the end of the lead.

(2) When at the end of the lead, remind your dog to Stay, then—

(3) Unceremoniously drop your lead on the ground. *Drop* the lead, *don't place* it. Step on the end of the lead.

(4) Remind your dog to Stay and take one step back.

(5) Remind your dog to Stay again and take another step back.

(6) If your dog breaks, immediately step on your lead with either foot and chastise. Increase the time until the dog is staying a full two minutes in the Sitting position, and five minutes in the Down position at this increased distance.

THE FINISH

In this exercise you are going to teach your dog to go to the Heel position instead of you doing it. This routine is accomplished when your dog is Sitting directly in front of you with its nose in front of you close to, but not touching, your knees. This puts your dog in the correct position to execute this maneuver. In order to teach your dog to do the Finish, do as follows:

(1) Step in front of your dog so that it is no farther than six inches from you.
(2) Grasp all the lead in your right hand close to the snap.
(3) Use your dog's name and the command "Heel."
(4) Simultaneously administer a sharp jerk in a backward direction with your right hand, and take two steps backward commencing with the right foot.
(5) At the conclusion of the second step, switch the lead, which you still hold close to the snap, from your right hand to your left hand *behind* your back.
(6) Take two steps forward by leading off with your right foot and give the command to Heel a second time. Accompany this maneuver with a sharp jerk parallel to the ground in a forward direction.
(7) While moving forward, switch the entire lead from your left hand to your right hand. Still hold the lead close to the snap, preparing to make your dog sit.
(8) As you come to a halt, issue the command to Sit, and with your right hand jerk up while your left hand presses down on your dog's tail set.
(9) Praise your dog profusely, both verbally and physically.

Step 4 of the Finish: Take two steps back as you give a quick jerk on the lead in the same direction.

Step 5 of the Finish: After stepping back, switch the lead to your left hand, behind your back.

Step 6 of the Finish: Command "Heel" as you take two steps forward and give a quick jerk with the lead.

Step 7 of the Finish: To get ready to do the Sit, shift the lead to your right hand.

Step 8 of the Finish: Pull up on the lead, push down on the dog's hindquarters with your left hand and command "Sit."

54

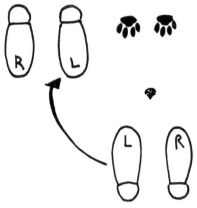

The Stand, showing the handler stepping back to the dog's side.

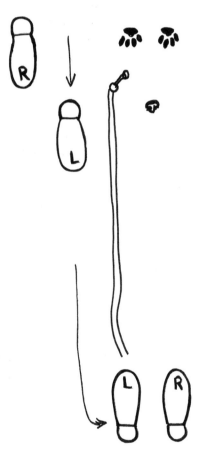

The Stand, with the handler a lead's length away.

THE STAND

In the United States you will have to do this exercise when the dog is off lead. If you should ever enter a competition in Canada, you will have to do this exercise on lead. The difference is a subtle one. In order to go through the exercise, do the following:

(1) Place your dog in a Standing position as I have described.
(2) Once your dog is quietly Standing in front of you, remind it to Stay and step to the dog's side.
(3) Drop the lead to the ground except for the loop held in your left hand.
(4) Use the hand signal and give your dog the command "Stay."
(5) Leave your dog and go to the end of the lead.
(6) Turn to face your dog for at least thirty seconds.

BACK UP AND CALL YOUR DOG

This is another exercise that leads into the formal Recall exercise. It is important that you walk backward quickly, and that you do *not* tow your dog as if it were a wagon. The lead should not be tight at *any* time after the jerk has been applied. To perform this exercise:

(1) Command your dog to Stay in the Sitting position and go to the end of the lead.
(2) With your dog at the end of the lead, use your dog's name followed by the command "Come."
(3) Follow the command with a sharp jerk backward and a quick step backward. In other words, say the dog's name, jerk and say "Come."
(4) Continue the quick walk backward (almost at a slow run with some eager dogs) while gathering the slack in the lead hand over hand. Keep walking backward quickly for at least fifty paces.

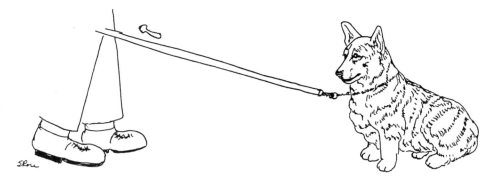

Steps 1–3 of Back Up and Call: Call "Come" after saying the dog's name and jerking quickly on the lead.

Steps 4 and 5 of Back Up and Call: Walk backwards quickly, gathering up slack in the lead. Encourage your dog verbally.

Step 7 of Back Up and Call: Guide the dog into you with the lead as you walk backwards.

As you come to a halt, hold the lead with your right hand, close to the snap.

At the Halt, pull up on the lead with the right hand and reach over the dog with your left hand to push down on the hindquarters. Command "Sit" simultaneously.

58

(5) As you are moving backward, encourage your dog with silly talk.

(6) When your dog begins to catch you, take the lead into your right hand so that you can begin to guide the dog into position directly in front of you. Your dog should be coming toward you with its nose close to, but not touching, your knees.

(7) You should cover the remainder of distance mentioned by constantly guiding your dog directly in front of you.

(8) As you come to a halt, with your dog immediately in front of you, be sure that your right hand is holding the lead close to the snap.

(9) As you administer a sharp jerk upward with the right hand, reach over the dog's back with the left hand and apply a sharp pressure downward as you command "Sit."

I cannot stress emphatically enough that the lead must be slack all the time, and you are simply gathering up the slack in the lead.

WAGGING ITS TAIL

Until now, with the inclusion of the last week of training in particular, you have been hard on your dog for breaking the Stay. This exercise is designed to offset this tough attitude. To accomplish this:

(1) Sit your dog.

(2) Leave your dog and go to the end of the lead as you would normally.

(3) While at the end of the lead, get your dog to wag its tail without breaking position, using any means you can.

(4) You can say anything that crosses your mind, use silly talk or attempt to trick the dog into wagging its tail.

(5) Basically, all dogs wag their tails, stumps or hindquarters when they are happy. Just make your dog happy.

(6) You can do anything you want to do—anything except

touch your dog. I don't care if you have to spit wooden nickels, just get the tail to move.

(7) Start heeling and do the same thing to get Fido's tail wagging while you are heeling with the dog.

This will get you thinking. Every dog will wag its tail depending on the behavior that you exhibit. It is pleasing to you if your dog is happily working with you. This exercise should effectively demonstrate the meaning of the word ''emote.''

7

Week Five—
Advancing:
Variations on
the Theme

$\mathbf{Y}$OU HAVE NOW completed the fourth week of training. When you practice all the lessons for the four full weeks of training, you will have completed twenty-eight hours of training. At this stage you are halfway through the training program.

(1) Stand and examine your own dog
(2) The left hand off the lead
(3) The circle return
(4) Down from the front
(5) The figure eight

Return to your dog, who should still be in the Stand position. Reach over and stroke your dog from head to tail.

"STAY"

Remind your dog to "Stay," and you return to Heel position, going around behind your dog.

STAND AND EXAMINE YOUR OWN DOG

In order to complete this exercise, do the following:

(1) Complete the exercise "Stand" until your dog is standing and you are at the end of the lead.
(2) Remind your dog to Stay, and then move toward your dog.
(3) Offer your dog the opportunity to sniff the back of your hand.
(4) While reminding your dog to Stay, reach over your dog and stroke the dog from head to tail.
(5) Remind your dog to Stay and step back to the end of the lead.
(6) Again, remind it to Stay and return around your dog as I have described previously.

THE LEFT HAND OFF THE LEAD

To prepare your dog for Heeling off lead, do the following:

(1) Remove your left hand from the lead before you begin a heeling routine.
(2) Use your dog's name and the command "Heel."
(3) Briskly step off on your right hand and commence a heeling routine.
(4) As you approach a turn, place your left hand on the lead, so that if the dog is not in the correct Heeling position, a jerk can be administered.
(5) The only time the left hand should be on the lead is whenever you have to perform a corrective jerk. Then you should immediately release it following the correction.
(6) From now on your left hand should be free of the lead except when you are planning a turn or pace change.
(7) Remember that you are still training and *not* testing your dog.

THE CIRCLE RETURN

In this particular maneuver you will be tempting your dog to break position, so be prepared for it. This exercise should be done in the Sitting, Down *and* Standing positions to be effective. Perform it in the following manner:

(1) Leave your dog and go to the end of the lead.
(2) Keep the lead in both hands, then return all the way around your dog, remaining a distant length of the lead from the dog on your first circle.
(3) As you complete one full circle, remind Princess to stay, and complete another circle one pace closer to your dog.
(4) Complete five entire circles, ever-diminishing in circumference. You should be walking closer to your dog with each new circle. Remind your dog to Stay after each of the circles. In other words, you are returning in a spiral pattern.
(5) Should your dog break position at any time, complete the number of circles remaining. For instance, if Princess breaks position after three circles, you still have two more to do successfully.

Use the word "no" the moment the dog breaks position and put her back in the correct position. Continue to complete the remaining number of circles. Don't start all over again.

DOWN FROM THE FRONT

Now you will understand the importance of raising your right hand when giving the command to go down. In case your dog can't hear a command when heading toward you and must cross a noisy road to get to you, it is wise to have your dog trained to know that the raised hand means "Hit the dirt." The dog's life may depend on this signal. This is how to accomplish a Down from the front:

(1) Sit your dog.
(2) Step in front so that your dog's nose is close to your knees.

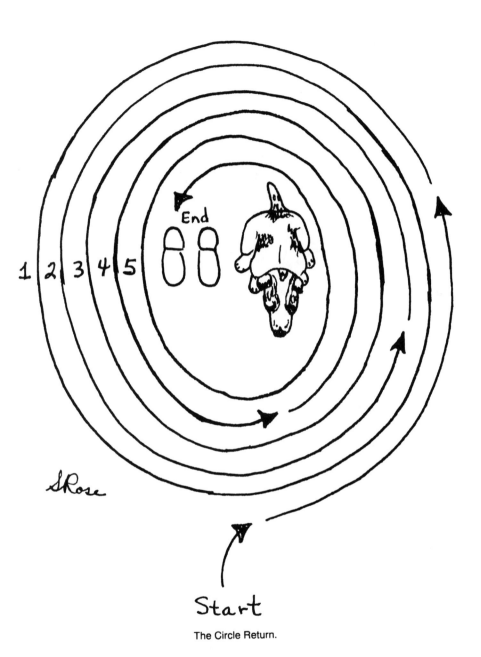

1 2 3 4 5

End

Start

The Circle Return.

SRose

When teaching the Down command from the front, step in front so that your dog's nose is close to your knees.

Drop to your left knee, hold the lead close to the snap and give a jerk downward.

66

(3) Place all the lead into your left hand close to but not on the snap.

(4) As your right hand goes up, command your dog to Down. Do not use its name.

(5) Drop to your left knee and administer a jerk downward with your hand clasping the lead close to the snap.

(6) Praise Princess when she is down.

(7) Command your dog to Stay and step to the side of your dog.

(8) Praise your dog.

THE FIGURE EIGHT

None of the exercises already taught are as important as the figure eight. If your dog will Heel properly off lead when you are walking in a figure eight pattern around two obstacles that are about eight feet (two and a half paces) apart, she will Heel anywhere. In order to perform the figure eight, you either have to find two obstacles that are about eight feet apart (such as two parking meters or cones, two streetlights, two garbage cans or two trees), or you can set up two obstacles such as pylons or stakes that are about two and a half paces apart.

Insist on a good Heeling position when you execute your figure eight pattern around the posts. When you move past the right-hand post, it will be necessary for your dog to Heel at a faster pace because she has to move in a larger circle than you do, but as you move around the left-hand post she has to Heel at a slower pace because the dog must move in a smaller circle than you do.

If you have a fast-moving dog that has a tendency to forge ahead of you, start the figure eight heeling around the right-hand post. If your dog is a bit on the slow side, start the figure eight around the left-hand post.

Perform this exercise at the normal, slow and fast paces, and intersperse a few about-turns as well. Anticipate your dog's attempt to slow down around the right-hand post and be prepared to administer a sharp jerk forward with a lot of silly talk. Prepare to administer a jerk backward when passing around the left-hand post.

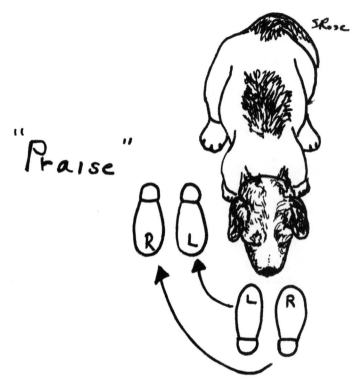

"Praise"

Command your dog to "Stay" in the Down position while you step back to the side of your dog, in the Heel position.

Steps 1–5 of the Figure Eight.

Don't adapt your pace to your dog, otherwise she will be training you. To perform this exercise, first set up your figure eight obstacles and then:

(1) Begin with your dog in the Heeling position between the two posts. You are not facing either post. In fact, you are at a right angle to both.

(2) Plan the initial direction in which you are going to travel around the posts (right or left).

(3) Use your dog's name and the command to Heel. With a sharp jerk, start with your right foot heading in the direction you have selected.

(4) Pass around the two posts twice, then halt and make your dog Sit. Again pass around the two posts twice but at a slow pace. Halt and make your dog Sit. Pass around the posts once again, but this time at a fast pace. Halt and make your dog Sit.

(5) Heel around the next post, about-turn, and repeat steps three and four around the posts in this new direction.

At this stage in training you have completed all the exercises for the first five weeks. After you have completed the fifth week of training, you will have practiced for thirty-five hours. This brings you past the halfway point in your training, and the following points should be kept in mind.

POINTS OF TRAINING

(1) All dogs under six months of age are puppies and have yet to mature both mentally and physically. It is very easy to bore a dog at this stage of training. This can be recognized by sluggishness and a browbeaten appearance when the dog is working. To avoid this do the following:

A. Keep your training sessions short.
B. Vary the exercises as much as possible.
C. Don't train when you are angry.

D. Praise your dog *only* when it does something correctly and well.
E. Use a tidbit of food as a reward if you want—dogs will become more responsive.
F. Work your dog as quickly as possible in order to maintain interest and attention. With a puppy the attention span is very short.
G. Don't get into the habit of practicing extensively the exercises your dog performs well. Instead, practice those things the dog doesn't do well—these are the things that need practice.
H. Don't increase the length of a training session. Instead, increase the number of short sessions held during each day.

(2) Dogs that are over six months of age are maturing quickly, and the older they become, the more habitual their behavior becomes. At the commencement of their training animals over three years of age will require corrections of undesirable behaviors that have been learned over a lifetime.

In order to avoid many problematic behaviors before they become habitual, serious training should start during this period of maturation. The older dog can sustain an hour of training with ease, as long as it is a fast-paced training session.

(3) *Always, always* end your training sessions with an exercise that you know your dog will do well so that you can praise lavishly. In this manner the dog will most easily remember the last thing that happened. If you do this your dog will look forward to the next training session with great anticipation.

(4) The training collar is simply an extension of your lead, which permits you physical control of your dog at all times. Your dog should always be kept on a slack lead so that a sharp jerk may be used to regain your dog's full attention. A tight lead will only result in choking your dog continually and all this accomplishes is physical abuse of your dog.

(5) *Never, never* command your dog to do something that you are not prepared to enforce or praise. *If you know that you'll be unable to enforce the command, don't issue the command.*

Note: Your dog is first a pet, and should be treated as a pet. Reward Princess when she performs well, and don't reward her when she doesn't.

TRAINING AREAS

At this stage of training you should change the training area from a nice quiet distraction-free area to one that has some distractions in the form of people, cars, etc. An excellent area would be at the end of a shopping plaza (mall) after most of the retail stores have closed, so that the only store open may be the grocery store at the end of the plaza.

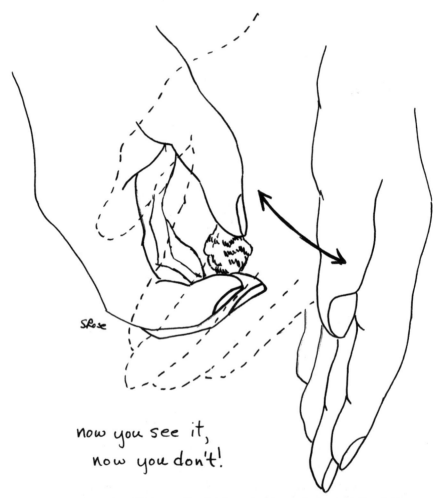

now you see it,
now you don't!

Food rewards work well because the dog is excited to receive a special treat. However, it is not wise to always hold the food so that your dog can see it.

8

Week Six—
Using Food Rewards

YOU ARE ABOUT to commence the sixth week of training with your dog. For this stage of training you will require food. The food you will be using is considered a "primary reinforcer" because it fulfills a biological need.

The selection of the type of food is of crucial importance. It should not be dog food of any kind. The best kind of food depends on what it is that your dog really enjoys, and you should take a little time discovering just what it is that your dog really likes. You want the kind of food that your dog would "kill" for.

This food will be used not to provide a meal, but to serve as a reinforcer for something done well. The praise will act as a secondary positive reinforcer. To obtain the greatest effect the praise should be administered immediately before the primary reinforcer (food). This simply means that you give the praise followed by the food. The closer in time that both are given as the result of the dog's reaction to the command, the faster the dog will learn.

The quantity is described in this manner. Most dogs seem to

have an affinity toward frankfurters or hot dogs that contain garlic. They also like chicken, roast beef or cheese. Take one hot dog and cut it into twenty slices. Take each slice and divide it into four quarters. Each of these pieces can be used as a positive reinforcer (treat) for having accomplished the necessary task at hand.

The primary reinforcer should not be something that takes time to chew; instead it should be such that the dog simply takes the treat and consumes it with one gulp. It should be a convenient size that allows you to carry several pieces in your shirt pocket. Later, I will describe where and when you use the food.

The exercises you have to practice during this week of training are as follows:

(1) Sit while in motion
(2) Diminish the Finish
(3) Step back and call your dog (in motion)
(4) Recall using food
(5) Sit and Down Stay with lead beside the dog

SIT WHILE IN MOTION

Time yourself so that you perform in the following fashion:

(1) Issue the command to Sit when your right foot touches the ground.
(2) Grasp the entire lead in both hands close to where the left hand was holding the lead.
(3) As the left foot comes up to the right foot when halting, administer a sharp jerk upward with both hands.
(4) With your peripheral vision, observe what your dog is doing as your left foot comes up to the right foot.
(5) If by the time you say, "one thousand and one," your dog is beginning to sit voluntarily *do not* administer the jerk.
(6) Should your dog not sit even with the two-handed jerk, then release your left hand from the lead, give the com-

mand a second time and jerk up with your right hand while depressing the dog's rump with your left hand.

(7) Once your dog is sitting, give praise *enthusiastically*.

DIMINISH THE FINISH

Until now you have been taking two steps back, switching the lead from your right hand to your left hand behind your back, and taking two steps forward, culminating the exercise with the command "Sit" and making your dog sit.

At this stage in your dog's training this is going to change to the following:

(1) As before, when your dog is sitting immediately in front of you, use a name and the command to Heel.
(2) Use a sharp jerk in the backward direction as you start to step back with your right foot.
(3) After one pace, switch the lead from your right hand into your left hand behind your back.
(4) Use the command to Heel a second time.
(5) Take one step forward on your right foot and place all the lead into the right hand by grasping it below the left hand.
(6) As your left foot comes up to your right, make your dog sit.

STEP BACK AND CALL YOUR DOG (IN MOTION)

While you have your dog heeling beside you, do the following:

(1) As you are moving, place the loop of the lead into your right hand.
(2) Use your dog's name and the command "Come."
(3) Release all of the lead, with the exception of the loop held in your right hand.
(4) Use a sharp jerk in the backward direction.
(5) Start walking backward quickly.

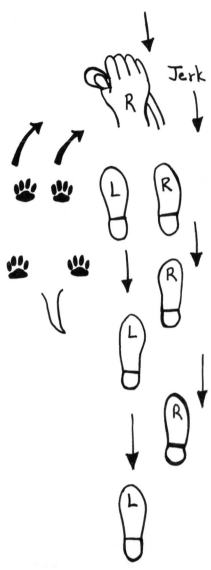

To Step Back and Call your dog, as you are heeling *and* with the lead in your *right* hand holding the loop, give a jerk, release the length of the lead and begin moving backward quickly.

As you come to a stop facing your dog, command your dog to Sit, press on the dog's rump with your left hand and jerk the lead up with your right hand.

(6) As you are moving backward, take up the slack in the lead hand over hand until you have almost reached the snap on the lead.

(7) Continue backing up about fifty paces while gently guiding the dog directly in front of you. This is similar to "Back up and call your dog," as done in lesson 4.

(8) When you stop walking backward, reach over the dog's back with your free left hand.

(9) As you come to a halt, command the dog to Sit.

(10) Press down on the dog's rump with your left hand and jerk up with the right hand.

RECALL USING FOOD

You will use food in your training for the first time in this exercise. The food you have selected must be used properly. There are a thousand ways of using food incorrectly, but only one way of using it properly. If you start by using it properly, you will save yourself a lot of training problems later. To use it correctly:

(1) Give your dog a tidbit for doing nothing—just for putting up with you all this time.

(2) Wait until your dog has eaten it. Show your dog a handful of food before giving the command and hand signal to Stay.

(3) Leave your dog and go to the end of the lead.

(4) Remind your dog to Stay as you reach the end of the lead, where you will turn to face the dog.

(5) Drop your lead on the ground and stand on the end of it.

(6) Reach out with the food.

(7) Use the dog's name and give the command to Come.

(8) Give the food the very moment your dog arrives in front of you.

(9) While the dog is eating the food, reach down and pick up your lead with the right hand.

(10) Once your dog has eaten the food, reach over her back

with your left hand, give the command to Sit, jerk up with your right hand and push down on the dog's rump with your left hand.

(11) During the week, as Princess becomes more and more certain of receiving the food, increase the distance you leave her.

(12) Do not increase the distance to more than fifty paces from the dog.

SIT AND DOWN STAY WITH LEAD BESIDE THE DOG

When you leave your dog in either a Sitting or Down position (not on a Stand), first place your lead on the ground between you and the dog. Begin by leaving Princess at the following distances: three paces, then six paces, then nine paces, then twelve paces, then fifteen paces.

Should your dog break position at any time, it is crucial that you chastise her and in no uncertain terms return the dog to position.

Place her back on lead and start over again. Increase the time you have left your dog at each of these distances from half a minute to one minute, to one and a half minutes, to two minutes, to two and a half minutes, to three minutes. Further increase the time in thirty-second intervals to five minutes.

At this stage in your training *consistency* is the most important characteristic that you can employ in order to achieve maximum results.

9

Week Seven— Checking on Progress

AT THIS STAGE of your training you are getting close to completing the training program. The progress of your dog should be very apparent. This week of training includes:

(1) Lead over-the-shoulder Heeling
(2) Sitting in motion (silent)
(3) Straighten the Sit
(4) Stand for examination
(5) Recalls and food for sitting
(6) Stays off lead

LEAD OVER-THE-SHOULDER HEELING

Until now the lead has always been held in your hands. Now we will start the first maneuver that leads to off-lead Heeling. To accomplish this:

Lead Over the Shoulder Heeling: Adjust the lead so it is slack.

(1) Place the lead across the back of your neck with the loop held over the thumb of your right hand.
(2) Adjust the lead so it is slack.
(3) Allow your left hand to swing freely at your left side.
(4) Use the dog's name and the command to Heel.
(5) Step off on your right foot with no jerk on the lead. If your dog doesn't Heel immediately with you, place your left hand back on the lead, enabling you to administer the sharp jerk.
(6) Every time you wish to make any kind of turn or to change your speed, grasp the lead with your left hand in anticipation of giving a jerk.

It is important that you don't try to test your dog at this stage. Before making a change in direction or speed, put the left hand on the lead and use it as if the dog had not received any training. Execute the sharp jerk as usual.

SITTING IN MOTION (SILENT)

In this exercise you do the "two-handed jerk" again when you come to a halt, except you do *not* make a sound. Take particular care in observing your dog as the left foot is brought up to the right foot. If your dog starts to sit, do not employ the jerk. In a sense you are beginning to test your dog's responses.

STRAIGHTEN THE SIT

Until now you have been content if your dog sat whenever you halted. Not anymore. If Star is not sitting exactly in the same direction as you are facing when you come to a halt, she is sitting crooked. The problem can be corrected at this stage of training before it becomes an insurmountable problem. Correct a crooked Sit in this fashion:

(1) Out of the corner of your eye observe how your dog is going to Sit. If your dog is going to be crooked, then before her bottom touches the ground—

(2) Give the command to Heel once more and take a quick step forward and physically make the dog Sit again.

(3) Continue to do this every time your dog even begins to Sit crooked, even if you have to go through this maneuver several times. Once the dog is sitting straight, take her through a long heeling routine as a reward.

STAND FOR EXAMINATION

Now you require the aid of a second person who is a stranger to the dog. This is a must. In a shopping plaza there are normally several people who are more than willing to accommodate you. All you have to do is ask if they would mind petting your dog a few times. If they ask you why, explain that you need their assistance as you are training your dog. If they agree, then:

(1) Use the ritual to place your dog in a Standing position.

(2) Instruct your assistant to start the petting after you have given the command and the signal to Stay, just as you did when you examined your dog.

(3) Once they have concurred with your request return around your dog.

RECALLS AND FOOD FOR SITTING

When you started to teach your dog the Recall, you physically made Star come and sit when she arrived. She then received a treat just for coming to you.

That is about to be changed. The reward will be given to your dog for sitting. The exercise is accomplished in this fashion:

(1) Once you have your dog sitting at your side, remove the lead and place it around your neck. This will free your two hands.

(2) Do not use your dog's name. Give your dog the com-

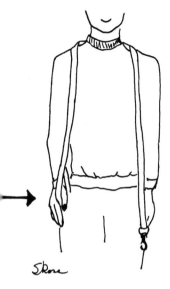

Lead positioned Over the Shoulder to begin off-lead Heeling: Place the lead around the back of your neck, with your right thumb through the loop.

Remove the lead from your dog and place it around your neck when using food for sitting.

Snap the lead behind your back to begin stays off-lead.

Snapped behind the back

mand and the signal to Stay and then walk a distance of about ten paces.

(3) Every four steps turn your head to look at your dog and repeat the Stay command.

(4) Take special care to repeat the Stay command when you turn to face the dog. By now she knows you have the treat. Without the reminder to Stay, she might anticipate the Recall command and break position to come to you.

(5) At the prescribed distances (ten–fifteen–twenty paces) wait for ten to thirty seconds, then use your dog's name and follow it with the command to Come.

(6) For a fast-moving dog, give the command to Sit when she is a few paces away from you, thus giving Star a chance to sit before she bumps into you or runs past you. For a slow-moving dog, give the command to Sit when she is close to you so she can sit in front of you.

(7) Hold the tidbit about six inches above Star's head and, *if necessary*, again give the command to Sit.

(8) The moment her hindquarters touch the ground in front of you, give the treat.

(9) If she starts to go past you, don't step in front of her; *instead—*

(10) Hold the food in front of her nose and entice her to return to sit in front of you. *Don't move your feet.*

STAYS OFF LEAD

Take the lead off your dog while she is sitting beside you. Place the lead around your shoulders so that you have freedom of both hands and arms, then:

(1) Give the signal and the command to Stay.

(2) Leave your dog five–ten–fifteen paces while attempting to reduce the reminders to Stay.

(3) Increase the Stay time by ten-second intervals until she will Stay for two minutes while sitting and five minutes in

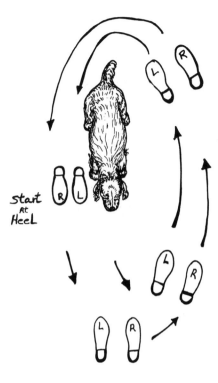

Start
At
Heel

During the off-lead Stay, leave your dog lying down at Heel position and stand several paces away, facing your dog. Face your dog, repeating the Stay command. Return back around your dog, stopping at Heel position.

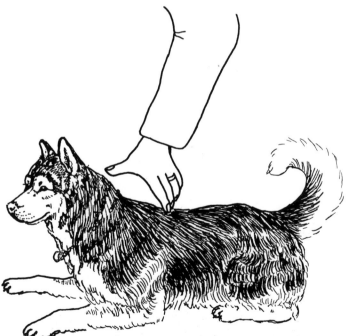

For off-lead Stays, prepare to use your open left hand to place the dog back in position.

the Down position. Remember that it is far nicer to praise for staying a short time than it is to scold for breaking after a longer time. Time is more important than distance.

(4) While the dog is lying down, prepare for what is going to happen next.

(5) When you return around the dog, open your left hand between the thumb and forefinger.

(6) When you get beside your dog, prepare to use that open left hand just behind the shoulder blades, as shown here.

(7) Remind your dog to Stay.

(8) On the spot, jump in the air about six inches.

(9) Should your dog pop up as a result, quickly use that left hand to unceremoniously place your dog back down, accompanied with lavish *praise*.

10

Week Eight—
No Strings Attached

---

(1) Lead trailing
(2) The Finish using food
(3) Recall with a target

When your dog has been heeling beside you, you have been aware of its responses whenever you started to make a turn in motion. If you notice that your dog is endeavoring to anticipate the jerk on the lead, it is ready for this lesson. If not, then your jerks have been ineffective and you'll have to repeat some of the previous lessons until you can see this conscious response to the jerk.

So far, you have placed your left hand on the lead in order to anticipate possible problems in heeling. In this manner you have been able to provide the corrective jerks when required. The left hand and arm should have been moving in a natural manner while

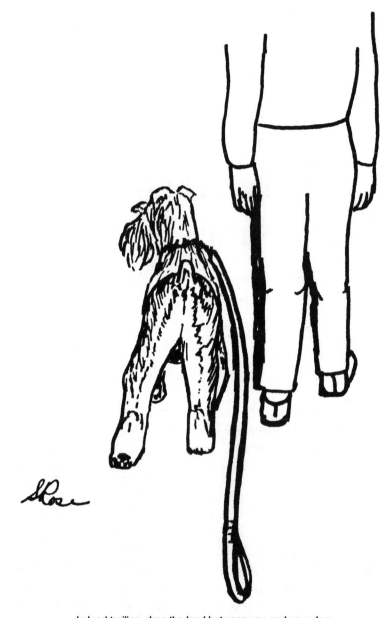

In lead trailing, drop the lead between you and your dog.

you moved with your dog. Now you have come to the moment in which you will test your dog.

LEAD TRAILING

When your dog is heeling in a straight line, prepare yourself mentally for this next step. In order to accomplish this feature of the heeling process, perform the following:

(1) Make an about-turn, and after you make the turn, apply a popping jerk.

(2) Surreptitiously, drop your lead between you and your dog. Make sure the lead is on the ground between your dog and yourself.

(3) Make another about-turn and use your left hand to slap your left side, accompanied with a vigorous command to the dog to Heel.

(4) Have your dog Heel beside you in this fashion, using a great deal of silly talk to obtain and keep your dog's attention on you. Use your left hand to pat your left side, especially when executing turns.

(5) *If* it becomes *necessary, use a tidbit* held in your right hand to keep the dog's attention on you while heeling.

(6) Should your dog begin to move ahead of you, reach out with your left foot and simply step on the lead while you are heeling. When this happens, the dog probably will receive the hardest jerk experienced up to this point in the training. Even after stepping on the lead, keep on walking and execute your turns. When you start to make a turn, pat your left side and emote as you give the command to Heel.

Allowing the lead to trail in this manner is similar to working the dog off lead. Being off lead or with the lead trailing should be treated as a privilege, not as a right. Any misbehavior should result immediately in you picking up the lead so that you can make any necessary corrections. You cannot correct your dog effectively when the lead is either off or trailing.

The trailing lead should be reserved as a treat, not as a regular feature of your heeling program.

THE FINISH USING FOOD

Up until now, the Finish has always been performed on the lead, with one or two steps back accompanied by a sharp jerk, and one or two steps forward accompanied by another sharp jerk.

Now there is no jerk and no lead. Instead, perform the exercise in the following manner:

(1) Step in front of your dog as usual for the Finish.
(2) Remind your dog to Stay and drop the lead in front of you.
(3) Step on the lead so your dog cannot move away from you.
(4) Take a piece of food between the thumb and forefinger of your right hand.
(5) Place the food directly in front of your dog's nose.
(6) Use your dog's name and the command to Heel.
(7) Take one step back on your right foot, while maneuvering the food in front of its nose, as you would dangle a carrot in front of a donkey's nose to make a donkey move.
(8) Entice your dog to move up to your right side.
(9) Behind your back, switch the food from your right hand to your left hand, coaxing the dog to follow the food as you move it.
(10) Take one step forward while again giving the Heel command.
(11) As your dog comes up to your left-hand side from behind you, give the Sit command and hold the food directly over the dog's head.
(12) With your right hand, give your dog the food for sitting.

This exercise should be incorporated into the various Recall exercises that have been covered. It may be convenient to carry

For the Finish off-lead, lead the dog around behind your back by switching the food from your right hand to your left hand.

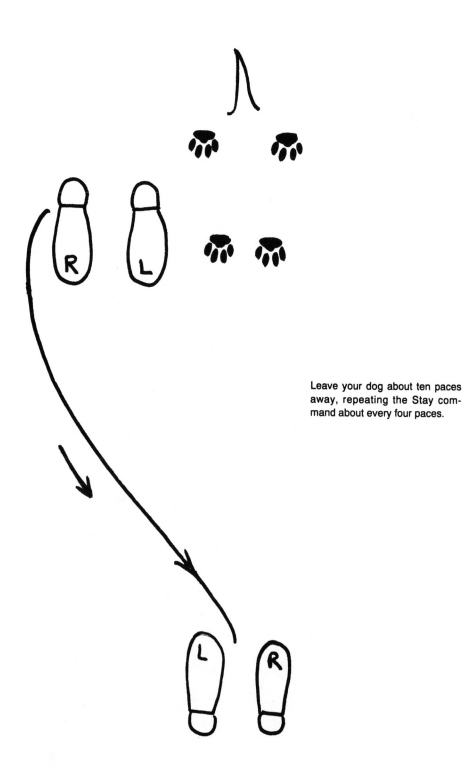

Leave your dog about ten paces away, repeating the Stay command about every four paces.

several tidbits of food in your pocket. This makes it handy when using the food during the Recall exercise.

RECALL WITH A TARGET

Up to now you have been giving your dog the food for coming to a sitting position in front of you. The food will still be used, but now in a different manner.

At this stage of training your dog knows that you have the food when you call him to Come. There might be a tendency to anticipate the Recall when you turn to face the dog. This is why it is imperative that you remind Fido to Stay every few paces as you leave. It is especially important to look directly at the dog when reminding him to Stay. Make it a definite command. It is equally important to repeat the command as you turn to face him during this exercise. To complete this exercise, do the following:

(1) Initially, leave your dog about ten paces, again reminding him to Stay about every four paces as you leave.

(2) As you are leaving, place your treat between the thumb and forefinger of your right hand. Before turning to face Fido, cover your right hand with your left hand.

(3) As you turn to face the dog, give a reminder to Stay and flash the food to remind Fido you still have it. In this manner the dog will see the covered right hand contains the treat. This will appear as a "target" to the dog.

(4) After about twenty to thirty seconds, use your dog's name and the command to Come.

(5) When your dog arrives in front of you, evaluate whether or not the Sit is going to be close enough to you and straight in front of you.

(6) If not, pretend you are a "flasher." That is, simply flash the treat that is cupped in your right hand in front of you, take a quick step back and again give the command to Come.

(7) Continue to repeat this until your dog is sitting close to you and straight in front of you, *then* give the dog the treat.

At this stage of the training you have covered all of the techniques required to complete the training of a dog at the Novice level. After fifty-six hours of training, and during the ninth week, it is time to test your dog's progress to see how much has been learned.

11

Problem Solving

COMPETITIVE OBEDIENCE is one field of training that the owner of a purebred dog might aspire to enter. No matter what area of training a person wishes to pursue, whether for competitive Obedience or for a better behaved pet, some problems will be encountered along the way. I firmly believe that both the handler and the dog must *enjoy* the experience of training; once the enjoyment is gone, whether in the training or in the exhibiting of a dog, it is time to look elsewhere for some other source of enjoyment.

I have heard the term to "force break" dogs used by some trainers, and once I have perceived what they are doing to their dogs, I understand just what they mean. I cannot comprehend the enjoyment they receive from this kind of training.

Some people are looking for the high score in Obedience Trials, while others are shooting for the perfect score of 200 points. I can understand this because when I enter a licensed Obedience Trial I certainly don't anticipate receiving a low score as the result of my dog's efforts; however, while the perfect score is 200 points, a qualifying score is 170 points, or 85 percent of the points allocated.

The competition-minded individual should realize that 170 points is a passing score, and a high score is icing on the cake. It saddens me to see the poor attitude of a handler who is disgruntled because a dog did not perform to the trainer's high expectation. To watch an exhibitor exit from an Obedience Trial and witness the dog being punished because of a disappointing performance disheartens me.

Regardless of why a person decides to train a dog, *there is no reason why both the handler and the dog—especially the dog—should not enjoy the training experience.*

During the training session a good trainer provides the motive for the dog, which generates a positive attitude in the dog. This attitude is displayed in everything the dog does and is reflected in the dog's facial and body expression, as well as in its movements.

Nothing can make people end up with egg on their faces the way dogs can. On the other hand, there is nothing that can give as much pleasure as seeing a well-motivated performance given by a well-trained dog that really is enjoying what it is doing. But getting the dog to this point takes hard physical labor and you will run into problems when you are training a dog to give this robust performance. Don't ever expect the dog to do something that it hasn't been trained to do.

Now I will endeavor to highlight some of the common problems that people encounter when trying to train their dogs during the first eight weeks of training. I will also cover other common types of problematic behaviors that people constantly ask about. There are many more than I will list here, but these are the most common.

HAIR LOSS AROUND THE COLLAR AREA

This is a typical problem that usually manifests itself at about the third week of training. What in fact is happening is that the handler isn't applying a *sharp*, quick jerk. Instead, there is a tug-of-war between the handler and the dog. The see-saw action of the collar results in the hair being worn away by the sliding action of the collar. In order to avoid this hair loss, you have to learn how to apply the sharp jerk. You might think that by going to a fabric type of collar you will reduce the hair loss your dog is experiencing—it may help somewhat, but the basic problem will remain unsolved.

The lead *must* be slack at all times, except when the jerk is applied, at which point it goes tight, then *immediately* loosens. Using a fabric collar instead of the stainless steel training collar is similar to the situation in which someone stops driving a car in order to avoid an automobile accident. It will work because you won't have an accident, but at what cost? No more driving anywhere.

THE HANDLER'S BLISTERED HANDS

A typical problem is blistered hands. A novice handler will sometimes discover that the lead cuts into the palm of the left hand below any rings. Or perhaps long fingernails will dig into the palm of the hand. These indicate that a lead is being handled incorrectly. In order to protect their hands, handlers often attempt to compensate by wearing gloves, especially when the handler attempts to use a chain lead or a canvas lead. The canvas lead results in cuts similar to paper cuts that usually occur as the result of a tug-of-war. If you are dealing with a large dog, you'll lose the battle every time.

Ensure that the lead is made of leather, preferably a soft latigo type of leather. The lead should be ½ to ⅝ inch in width for the average size dog (30–140 pounds) and ¼ inch for the small dog (less than 30 pounds).

Make sure you aren't grasping the lead in your left hand behind the knuckles. Instead, grasp the lead in your left hand on the "heel" of your hand (up high on the palm of your left hand, just below your wrist). If you want a firmer grasp, then double the lead around the palm of your left hand. Under no circumstances should you grasp the lead between your fingertips. Once you have administered the sharp jerk, ensure that the lead goes slack. You cannot give a proper jerk when the lead is tight.

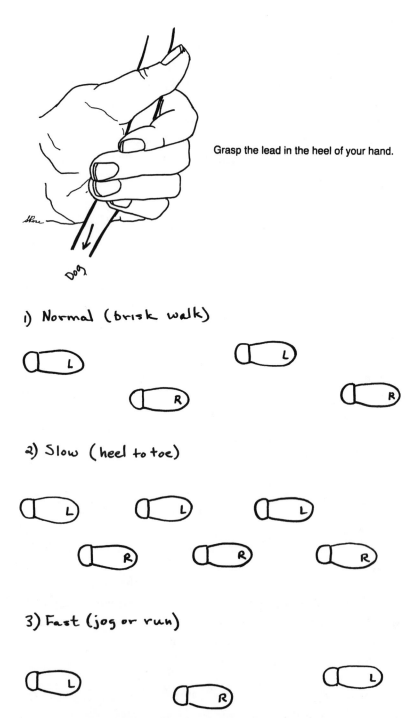

Grasp the lead in the heel of your hand.

1) Normal (brisk walk)

2) Slow (heel to toe)

3) Fast (jog or run)

For a dog that is heeling too closely, try a variation of speeds.

98

THE DOG HEELS TOO CLOSELY

At this stage in training your dog cannot be too close to you. When you start the second week of training, if this is a chronic condition:

(1) Let your dog select the direction and the speed it wants to move in, then respond to this by *doing the opposite*. Begin your heeling routines with a great deal of about-turns, circle rights and left turns—especially left turns.
(2) Start into a fast speed, then suddenly break into an about-turn followed by a "normal" speed.

NOT SITTING WHEN HALTING

This is a classic problem. If you come to a halt first *before* making your dog sit, the dog may brace his hind legs under him, after which it becomes almost impossible to make Fido sit. Even a small dog can brace.

The trick is to (1) jerk up with the lead, and (2) press down on the dog's hindquarters as you move to bring your left foot even with your right foot. In this manner Fido's hind legs are still in motion while you are taking the weight off his front end by applying the jerk applied directly upward—not backward. The pressure downward on the rump is minimal. You must administer the jerk up with your right hand while simultaneously pressing the hindquarters down with your left hand.

Make sure you have grasped the entire lead in your right hand *below* the position of the left hand before attempting the jerk upward so that it will be felt as a jerk. Use the flat palm of the left hand (fingers and thumb close together), with the fingers pointed toward the dog's tail, to press the hindquarters down.

LYING DOWN DURING THE STAY

A lot of dogs will lie down before you have the opportunity to step in front of them. If this happens during the initial training of the

Stay command, do a quick circle right on the spot and start your dog again. Do the same if it attempts to either Stand or Heel with you, but *do not* scold your dog since it hasn't learned the meaning of the command "Stay" yet (week two's lesson).

JUMPING ON THE HANDLER

If your dog tends to jump up on you, it is showing you affection, and it would be incorrect to scold. *The worst thing you could do is knee your dog in the chest for jumping on you.* If you do this you could cause physical injury even to the extent of rupturing the heart. Don't do it! There is an easier way to correct the situation that won't cause physical harm to you or your dog.

You want your dog to show affection for you, so praise Fido for jumping on you. He receives something "nice" for jumping on you, but now you have to take the niceness out of this act. You must show that you want the affection, but not in this manner. To stop this behavior:

(1) Coax your dog to jump on you.
(2) Reach down, taking one paw in each hand with your thumbs pointing up.
(3) Tell Fido how much you like him to jump on you, even praise him.
(4) Squeeze your hands around his pads and feet.
(5) When your dog begins to want to move away, you are starting to become effective.
(6) Keep him up for at least thirty seconds. Take a few steps while you look at your dog and say, "What's the matter? I like you up here."
(7) After the thirty seconds, release Fido and coax him to repeat the act again.
(8) If he attempts to nibble at your hands, bring his paws together and feed him his own paws. If he wants to chew something, let it be his own paws.

It's like telling a young child, "Don't touch the stove, you'll burn yourself." You can tell him a thousand times, and still he may

Curing your dog of jumping on you.

touch the stove—until he actually burns himself. Very quickly the dog learns that as much as you like to have him jump up, it becomes uncomfortable for him and the niceness is gone. He will learn quickly to jump up while he is three feet away from you, with his paws tucked away from you.

Do it yourself for a few days, then have a member of the family do it for a few days. Finally have a family friend do it to reinforce the lesson on several levels.

DIGGING IN THE YARD

Dogs dig because they usually receive some sort of satisfaction from doing so. Often they will dig in a flower bed because they are attracted by the bone meal mixed in the soil beneath the plants. In any case, you have to take the niceness out of the experience. There are two ways to accomplish this:

(1) Place some feces in the hole the dog has dug and cover it lightly with soil. Usually the dog will return to the same spot to resume digging. This remedy will give quite an unpleasant surprise.

(2) Should the dog persist, instead of feces, place some rose-bush cuttings or a four-to-six-inch length of chicken wire in the hole and cover lightly with sand. You will not have caused any harm, but the dog will discover by itself that this digging is unpleasant. In this fashion you will have removed the niceness from the act of digging.

SNAPPING AT PEOPLE

Most dogs will bite out of either fear or hostile aggression. The method used to correct the behavior will depend on the reason behind your dog's snapping.

The first type I will talk about is the one that bites out of hostile aggression. This dog can usually be identified by tail carriage, which is high, and ears, which are normally carried up and forward. When this dog growls, the mouth usually forms a circle around the front of the muzzle. The mouth, ear carriage and eyes give the impression that the dog is going to move forward. There is no doubt from the expression of the facial muscles that the dog is trying to move toward the person against whom the aggression is intended. There is no expression whatsoever of fear. This hostile behavior must be curtailed quickly. In order to do so, perform the following:

(1) Place a container filled with water (about a liter—neither hot nor cold) at a place where you expect the aggression to occur. A convenient container would be a plastic fruit juice pitcher with a handle.

(2) As soon as the dog appears to think about reacting in a hostile fashion, administer the entire container full of water directly in its face.

(3) Do not say anything. Neither a scolding nor a reprimand should accompany the water.

(4) The water has to be the result of the dog even thinking about being hostile. Do not use a water pistol, hose or other convenience.

Dogs are similar to humans in this respect. We all like water but not when it is delivered in this fashion. Picture, if you will, your attitude if you came around the corner of a building and were suddenly hit with a bucket of water. It would certainly dampen your enthusiasm quickly. A dog can fight water from a hose, or may even try to play with it. Water from a container is so abrupt that the dog doesn't have any opportunity to fight it. It is there—then it is gone. It is the shock value that you are counting on. This doesn't harm the dog in any fashion and it doesn't stain. However, it should be reserved for the truly hostile, aggressive type of dog.

The other type of biting is a reaction to fear, and the above technique should not be employed. It would only serve to make the dog more fearful. One can ascertain quickly whether a dog is in fact fearful by noting the facial expression. The eyes take on a wide-eyed expression so that the fear is very obvious. There could be many different reasons for the dog reacting in a fearful manner. This type of behavior needs reassurance. If you act in a hostile manner or scold the dog for fear, the treatment could easily backfire on you.

Instead, have someone else examine your dog, but make sure the person understands that eye contact should not be made with the dog. Eye contact is interpreted by many dogs as a challenge and it is met by the fight or flight response. At the same time have the person give the dog a treat. Some dogs become so fearful that food has no effect on them whatsoever. This is because the "protective drive" has been engaged along with the "flight" aspect rather than the "fight" condition. All other moods and drives will be completely subjugated. This will even manifest itself to the point that the dog will not accept the food under any condition.

Dogs have a psychological distance that they attempt to maintain from anything they perceive as a possible threat to their safety. It is called the "distance threshold." The brave dog maintains a very small distance while the fearful animal insists on a very large distance. A person that crosses this psychological distance represents a threat to the dog's well-being and the dog will attempt to move away to maintain the distance. Anything that the examiner does that threatens this distance, e.g., eye contact, will result in the protective drive being engaged.

Should this be the case, then have the examiner do the following:

(1) While the dog is in the Stand-Stay position, have the examiner walk a large circle around the dog, avoiding any eye contact and vocalization.
(2) While walking around the dog, have the examiner throw a piece of food in toward the dog.
(3) Let the dog break the Stay command to go after the food.
(4) Have the examiner tighten the circle until he or she is walking right up to the dog.
(5) After a few days of this, have the examiner offer the food to the dog without a pause and absolutely *no* eye contact.
(6) When the examiner has managed to reach a point where the food can be offered to the dog, have the examiner offer the food in the palm of the left hand while he or she scratches the dog between the ears with the right hand.

This entire process is part of what is known as "successive approximation" or shaping. In the case of the aggressive, hostile dog, you want to react in a manner that lets the dog know that you are the master of the situation. Temper this with the knowledge that the fearful dog needs your patience and understanding.

SITTING ON THE STAND EXERCISE

Every time you attempt to Stand your dog, it reacts by Sitting. To correct this, do the following:

(1) Step in front of your dog. Repeat the command to Stand. Lower your right hand, with the fingers extended but held close together. Check the dog's forward motion by allowing it to run into your open hand.
(2) If the dog continues to attempt to Sit, place the open right hand, palm down, on the inside of its left thigh.
(3) Use the fingertips of the open hand to increase pressure outward on its thigh.
(4) Do not attempt to grasp your dog in any fashion.

   If it is a case of gross disobedience, then grasp the dog by the cheeks and give a vigorous scolding with a meaningful "What the heck is this."

THE CONFORMATION STAND

Many people who own purebred dogs are concerned that their dogs will Sit instead of Stand when they halt in the Conformation competition ring. This is another wives' tale. Make sure that you leave your dog by stepping off on the left foot. It will begin to realize that this means to Stay, as opposed to when you step off on the right foot, which means that you want it to Heel.

When performing the Stand as described, the dog is walked into a Stand position and is given the command to Stand. By stepping in front of the dog, you are inhibiting the sitting reflex. Before the dog can Sit, you have stepped in front of it and walked it into a

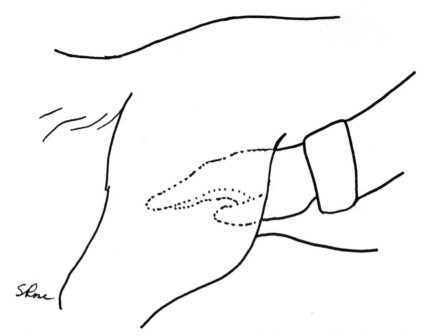

To *keep* your dog in the Stand, apply pressure on the dog's inner thigh with your right hand.

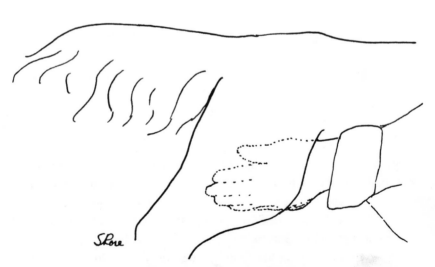

Preventing a sit during the Stand.

Stand. Also, during the Stand, the lead should never become tight. A tight lead is a signal for the dog to Sit.

I hear some people state that they won't obedience train their dogs because they want to go into Conformation first. A well-behaved dog is a pleasure to show in the Conformation ring.

DESTRUCTIVE BEHAVIOR

Many people find that their dog is destructive when left alone in the house. The dog either chews the furniture or your shoes, or tears the bedding or drapes apart. Invariably, the owner arrives home to find a dog that gives the appearance of having done something wrong. Obviously the owner is not pleased, especially since the evidence of the dog's destructiveness is in plain view. The dog may act as if it knows what it has done, but the dog does not know because it does not have a long-term memory. Your dog can probably tell from your actions that you are displeased but won't associate the mess with its action. In order to avoid this type of situation, *prevent access*.

When left alone, a dog probably suffers from boredom, and if left to its own devices, usually becomes destructive. The worst thing you can do is reprimand your dog after the fact. Dogs do not have a memory like we do and probably have no idea what was done to upset you. Your dog probably thinks that it is in trouble for having come to you in a pleased fashion. To correct the problem:

(1) Obtain a fiberglass crate (such as a ventilated airline crate).
(2) Leave the crate open at all times in a convenient room.
(3) Dogs have the tendency to look for places of refuge—a place that is out of the way—usually under something like a coffee table, a bed or even the dining room table. It becomes a "home away from home." Tempt your dog a few times to enter into the circle with a well-placed treat and leave the door to the crate open.
(4) Permit access to the crate all the time when you are home.

When you have visitors, it will be convenient for you to close the crate door. A small treat will encourage your dog to go into the crate when you first start to use it. Or, you may feed the dog in the crate with the door left open.

(5) If you go out for any length of time, close the door and latch it. Keep the dog in the crate while you are gone and simply open the door when you return. In this manner you have prevented access.

BATHROOM PROBLEMS AWAY FROM HOME

When you visit a friend's home with your dog, perhaps one of the first things your dog does is to urinate. Usually it doesn't leave a great amount, just enough to irritate both you and your friend. You'll probably discover that other dogs have been in your friend's home. Particularly if your dog is a male, this is quite normal, though irritating.

Your dog has probably smelled the presence of the other dogs and is simply urinating to place its own odor over the other dogs' odor. In this fashion it is being "territorial." You should realize this behavior might occur when visiting the home of friends who have other dogs in residence. To avoid this, don't bring your dog inside the house with you.

SKUNKED!

I can empathize with people who have had the misfortune of having their pets sprayed by a skunk. This has happened to my dogs while tracking during late summer evenings. First, let me say that you can forget about giving them a bath in tomato juice: It is messy and it doesn't work. The only preparation that does work is a douche product by Massengill™. This will remove most of the offensive odor, but every time the dog becomes wet, the residual odor will return until it eventually wears off!

108

MOUTHING THE LEAD

While heeling with Fido, he grabs the lead and mouths it almost as if in play. This interferes with the heeling exercise.

This is another classic problem. The dog is deriving pleasure from what the handler considers an undesirable action, and this must cease. You have to take the niceness out of it. To accomplish this:

(1) When the dog grabs the lead by mouth, remove the lead in no uncertain terms by jerking it out of his mouth. *Do not* say anything. The sudden unpleasantness will suffice.

BARKING AT THE NEIGHBOR'S CATS

This is another classic problem. The dog could be barking at the neighbor's cats, passing people, the mailman or the paperboy and will not stop, even when told to do so. Once again, the niceness has to be taken out of the action. The dog could be getting any of several different pleasures out of this action, and you have to do something that makes it more unpleasant than pleasant:

(1) Have a bucket of water handy somewhere near where you think the barking will take place.
(2) The moment the barking begins, walk out of the house and give the ''cease and desist'' command.
(3) Without any further to-do, take the bucket and walk near your dog.
(4) Throw the bucket of water on the dog as the result of the barking.
(5) As you administer the water, warn your dog that you are getting the water.
(6) After one week of this, change to a pitcher of water.
(7) After another week, change to a water pistol.
(8) Ensure that you precede the action by the warning each time.

(9) Remember, you cannot correct this behavior if you are not present. You can't expect the dog *not* to bark if you are not nearby. If you are away, it is only reasonable that your dog will bark. Also, remember that the water should be neither cold nor hot.

Soon you'll discover that the barking stops as soon as you give the warning.

JUMPING THE FENCE

This is a real problem, especially if you aren't at home to take the necessary action when the dog starts to jump the fence. You can forget about attempting to "boundary" train your dog, especially if your dog is now an adult animal. As a very young puppy, several weeks of age or younger, you might make some headway in teaching the pup where the property line is, but you might as well forget it with the average dog that is more than a few months of age. This is a "sin" that usually occurs when you are not at home to take the appropriate action, so the correction has to be administered when you are absent and at the right moment. To correct this sort of problem when you are not there, rather severe action may be an option. A battery-operated fencer consists of one wire around the top of your fence and the other end connected to the "hot" terminal of the fencer. The other end of the fencer (ground) is attached to a long nail into the ground. Use your water hose to water down this connection that leads into the ground and up to the base of the fence.

When you turn on the unit, the watered terminal provides one of the terminals and the hot wire becomes the other terminal. In order for your dog to jump the fence, the hind paws make contact with the water ($-$). The front paws make contact with the "hot" wire ($+$), and the dog receives a shock. This shock does not harm the dog, but if it attempts to jump over the fence, the shock is immediate.

The dog may attempt to climb over the fence once or twice, but that will be all and the correction will have been made while you are not present.

EATING STOOLS (COPROPHAGY)

This can be a frustrating and dirty habit to have to correct. It is more common than most people would like to admit. The reason for the problem can range from boredom to some sort of nutritional deficiency, and it is a concern about which veterinarians receive many questions. There is no real cure for this problem, but you can decrease its frequency somewhat by adding some fresh pineapple to the dog's diet. There is also a chemical that can be added which is more effective. This chemical can be purchased from a veterinarian by the trade name FOR-BID™. It is a highly purified crystalline edible protein fraction. Place a few slices of pineapple or the chemical in each regular meal, thereby supplying the digestive system with something that makes the stool taste unpalatable. Your dog will not care for this taste in the stools. If and when the dog does eat the stool, you have to catch it in the act and really lower the boom. Also, remember that if you pick up after your dog defecates, you will not be giving access to this habit.

RUSHING THROUGH OPEN DOORS

When you open the door, the dog bolts out the door before you can stop it. This is a common problem, especially before the dog has learned the meaning of the Stay command. Follow the sequences given to teach the Stay, but don't expect miracles before the command has been learned. Once it has been learned—and not before—arrange to have someone come to the door, and when the bell is sounded, take your dog over to the door and give a Down-Stay command while you answer the door. Be sure to heed the following advice:

(1) Leave your dog in a position where it can observe the helper come through the door once the door is *opened*. Insist that the dog stay in this position.
(2) Make sure that you can see your dog at all times and that it is no more than one pace away from you.

111

If the dog starts to break the command, scold and enforce the Stay. Once the helper has come inside, praise the dog. Then after the door has been closed, release the dog from the Stay command.

THE PRONG COLLAR

There is controversy about the use of the prong collar. I feel that it is an issue that will continue for some time, and therefore one that deserves mention in an Obedience book.

All Obedience equipment, if handled correctly by knowledgeable handlers has a place in dog training. The prong collar is a collar with blunt spikes. The prongs (spikes) are located on the inside of a steel link collar. When pressure is exerted by a jerk on the lead, the ends of each prong protrude from inside the collar and pinch the dog's neck and throat.

Improperly used, the prong collar can be an instrument of torture, especially in the hands of the uneducated handler. I have witnessed physical damage as the result of the use of a prong collar. I will not permit them in my Obedience classes. They are a poor excuse for one's inability to use a standard chain collar. I can only see their possible use in the hands of a frail seventy-or eighty-year-old who has an overactive dog of immense size and even then the collar should be used only under close supervision.

Anyone can learn how to properly use a standard steel chain collar, but it may take a little longer for some people and extra effort for others.

ELECTRONIC COLLAR

Much has been written about the electronic collar and I would be remiss if I did not mention it here. I don't feel that it is an appropriate collar for Obedience training any dog. Even the chronic barking dog does not require this. There are too many things that can cause the collar to "go off," and it is highly possible that the dog could receive a shock when an airplane passes over or when a truck with a faulty ignition system passes nearby. You have very little control over the operation of an electronic collar. Once again, it is a poor substitute for the physical labor good dog training requires.

This dog enjoys finding the stick, but . . .

. . . he will perform any trick or task willingly for this kind of praise from his owner.

12

Tricks

BASIC TRICKS that will amuse and amaze your friends while holding your dog's interest can be taught to most dogs without difficulty. Just a few of these are:

(1) Sit up and beg
(2) Shake a paw (right or left)
(3) Walk on hind legs
(4) Bang! You're dead
(5) Roll over
(6) Speak (give voice)

When you are training your dog, you are wise to have a small retinue of simple tricks that your household pet can do, even if it is only to show off your pet's knowledge. Learning to perform simple tricks always gives the dog's owner a small amount of pleasure and helps one's dog learn how to learn. The simple process of learning a trick introduces the pet owner to a technical term called "successive approximation," which means behavior shaping. This is usually accomplished by rewarding the animal's behavior with a positive reinforcer as it becomes closer and closer to the end result desired. In this manner the end result is achieved by shaping the wanted behavior in increments until the entire desired behavior is evidenced by the dog in training.

A dog can learn everything necessary through "inducive" training and the use of positive reinforcement. The trick to becoming successful at using inducive training is rather simple. Follow this format:

(1) First, come up with some action coupled with a command. Your action has to be designed to "lead" or to "trick" your dog into doing something that begins to approximate the action that you want from your dog. The dog's initial reaction need only be a small portion of the final desired result. The moment your dog executes a desired action, do two separate things in the correct order.

First, praise your dog with a simple "good," and second, administer a positive reinforcer, preferably a "primary" reinforcer. Keep the time between the action, the praise and the positive reinforcer as short as possible. You want the positive primary reinforcer and the praise to have the same weight. In other words, the dog will look upon the praise with as much gusto as the piece of food. The timing between the praise and the food is of critical importance.

(2) The reinforcer that has the greatest psychological impact on your dog will cause the most rapid learning to take place. This is the effect of the primary reinforcer, which, in its simplest terms, is whatever is required for survival of the species. One primary reinforcer you appeal to is the feeding drive.

Should you want to appeal to your dog's feeding drive you can appreciate the difference a piece of kibble would have in comparison to a steak. So the selection of food type plays an important role when selecting food as a reinforcer.

Praise, verbal (psychological) or a pat (physical), is by any definition secondary reinforcement for having accomplished something. Ideally you want the praise to take on the characteristics of the primary reinforcement and have the same effect. This is why the secondary reinforcement should be administered a moment *before* the primary reinforcement. This means in its simplest terms that the praise will possess the same motivational benefit as a treat.

116

SIT UP AND BEG

With your dog sitting in front of you, hold a treat above and slightly in front of the dog's head. As you slowly raise the treat, the dog will start to raise her front legs above the ground and attempt to balance on her haunches.

Continue doing this until your dog reaches out to seize the food. Each time she goes through this action, demand that she sit up higher and higher until Star is back on her hind legs and haunches before giving the praise and the food. During this action, don't forget to remind her to Stay and also give the command to Beg.

When she seizes the food, don't give it too soon. Allow Star to grab the food while you are holding onto the other end of it. Raise the food while she is hanging onto one end and keep repeating the command to Beg. While you are holding onto one end of the food, support the dog's weight on the food or your fingers.

Increase the length of time that the dog has to hold the food until she is on her haunches. The closer she comes each time to settling on her haunches and holding the position, give the praise and the food. As soon as Star starts to raise herself, begin to praise, but don't give the food until the entire action has been completed. In other words, she gets the food for successfully completing the desired action.

Some dogs, because of their breed, may find this more difficult to accomplish than other breeds. Some breeds find it physically easier to accomplish this than others, but they can all learn how to perform this trick.

SHAKE A PAW (RIGHT OR LEFT)

This is a trick most dogs learn at an early age. The impact usually comes from the command that is given by the dog's owner.

I would suggest that you use the command "Give me five" before you do anything else. At the same time or shortly after giving the command, reach down in front of your dog with your right hand extended in an open fashion in front of your dog. Be sure that your dog is in a sitting position in front of you. Reach down in front of your dog so that you can lightly tap the area between the pastern (wrist) and the elbow while repeating the command to "Give me five." You may have to increase the tap slightly on the front leg in order to get your dog to raise a paw.

The very moment that the paw starts to elevate, praise your dog with a "Good" and give a tidbit. Continue this action until the dog begins to raise the one paw consistently on the command. Then you can discontinue having to touch the leg when giving the command.

If your dog is consistent with one paw, then it is time to give the command "No, the other one," and with the appropriate hand, reach down in front of the dog and gently touch the other paw so that Star will begin to raise the other paw. Once again, praise the action but leave the food out unless your dog raises the correct paw.

Soon you will be able to alternately command your dog "Give me five" and "No, the other one," until your dog will offer one paw and then the other. By alternating the commands with "no, the other one," you can make this trick one that will cause observers to laugh with your dog and give the appearance that Star knows the difference.

WALK ON HIND LEGS

This is another trick that is more easily accomplished by certain breeds of dogs than others because of their physical construction. This consists of your dog raising herself onto her hind legs and hopping at your side while you are walking. A lot of people take their dogs for a walk, but in this trick she is being taught to go along for a walk while on her hind legs. This is the type of trick that a lot of circus-trained dogs perform beside their handlers.

Begin by sitting your dog at your left side while you give Star the command to Walk. Hold a piece of food in your right hand held across your body a few inches above your dog's head. Occasionally bring the food down to a point just above the nose while you start moving at a slow walking pace. Entice the dog to leap up to get the

118

food that you have offered by holding it just above the head. In the beginning allow her to be successful at reaching the food on the first jump. Now insist on two leaps before giving the food by holding it just outside of reach.

Every time you take a small step forward, command Star to walk. Now insist upon your dog taking more and more hops before successfully reaching the offered food. You can consider the dog as being trained to perform this trick when she remains on her hind legs when walking (hopping) for a distance of a dozen paces without having to return to all four feet. Time and practice will add to the time and distance that your dog will continue this activity.

BANG! YOU'RE DEAD

This trick is two separate exercises taught in successive order and couples with it a command that really puts the wow in the act. In order to gain the most rapid learning of this trick, you would be wise to first teach your dog the Down command from the front as has been described. Second, you will have to teach your dog that the right-hand forefinger pointing at her coupled with the command "You're dead" means to lie on her side.

First, step in front of your dog after giving the signal with your right hand coupled with the command to Stay. The dog will then be in a sitting position immediately in front of your knees. Have a treat held in your left hand. Hold it so that your fingers cover the treat reinforcer and your palm is facing down. Continue to remind Star to Stay while you point your finger at the dog with your thumb pointing upward—pretending it is a revolver. Administer the verbal command "Bang!" and simultaneously move your left hand and the food it is holding below the dog's nose. As she attempts to reach for the food, slowly entice her into moving downward.

In the beginning give her the food for moving downward even if it is only slightly. Successively, each time you attempt this maneuver, wait until the movement gets closer to the dog actually lying down before you praise and give the food.

By using this method of successive approximation you will be

119

able to wait until Star is completely down before rewarding with the food. In short order she will learn that the command "Bang!" is another command meaning *Down* especially when the right hand is used as a signal. This follows a simple rule of thumb that I like to use, namely, the right hand gives the signal and the left hand administers the reinforcing action whether that reinforcing action is positive or negative in nature.

Once lying down in front of you, it is time to start working on the second portion of the exercise. This is the command "You're dead," and have the dog on her side in front of you. Before you start this part of the exercise, switch the food from your left hand to your right hand. You will administer the food for this maneuver with the right hand. Normally, you administer the food with your left hand for most of the Obedience exercises, but this is one of the exceptions to this rule.

While the dog is lying in front of you, take your left hand and place it beside Star (on the right side) and command "Bang! You're dead" as you push the dog's shoulder to the right so that she is lying on her left side on the ground in front of you. At the same time, use the food now held in your right hand to slide it below her head so that you may administer it as the dog's head gets closer to the Down position.

ROLL OVER

This exercise is taught in a fashion similar to the "Bang! You're dead" exercise. First, Down your dog in front of you. Give the command "Over," and then start this sequence of events:

(1) With your right hand holding the food, place it in front of the dog's nose, palm facing downward.
(2) With your left hand, scratch your dog on the hindquarters.
(3) Very gently, stop scratching and place the treat under the dog's two front legs, and with a slow, upward motion rotate your dog's front legs so this action causes the dog's body to swing over to the other side. Continue to hold the food in your right hand by the dog's nose.

(4) Often, the simple action of scratching your dog's hind-quarters will cause it to rotate onto the other side.

(5) In either case, the moment that your dog starts to rotate, give the praise followed by the food. This is for starting the desired action.

If you want to be successful all the time, make certain your dog is always lying down in front of you when you give this command.

SPEAK (GIVE VOICE)

There are many different conditions that warrant your dog giving voice for one reason or another. In any case, the first thing you must do is get your dog to give voice on command. Later, the command could be given for any reason, even toward an intruder or a ringing telephone as Hearing Dogs do. Most dogs will start to give voice on their own (after they have reached sexual maturity) when a stranger comes to the door. Here the protective drive takes over and the reaction is quite a natural one. There are many cases when the dog refrains from giving voice. Here is how you teach your dog to give voice on command.

Start with your dog either sitting in front or beside you. Keep a small piece of food in your right hand in case your dog gives any sort of sound. Usually, in the beginning, the sound may be a simple "yipe" or even a flexing of the facial muscles that is observable by the trainer—in this case, you. The very moment this action is noted, the praise and the food should be administered. The trick here is to evoke the desired response after the command is given and to do that we employ a response that Pavlov termed the "startle response."

While your dog is motionless either beside or in front of you, stare at it without any movement whatsoever on your part. After a few seconds of this staring match, very suddenly and with a jerky motion toward your dog, command it to speak. Accompany this with a sudden jerking motion toward your dog with your left hand as if you are attempting to snap onto a fly sitting on its nose. You want this action to evoke a startle response from your dog.

Repeat this maneuver several times in an attempt to elicit a startle response on the part of your dog. The very moment that your dog gives out with any sort of sound or has even a change in facial expression, praise and administer the food.

It cannot be stressed enough that any sort of reaction on your dog's part be accompanied with the praise followed by the administration of the food. In this manner you begin to "shape" the type of behavior that you want to elicit from your dog. Soon that little movement of your dog's facial expression will grow into a full-sounding bark. The difficulty now becomes getting your dog to keep quiet.

13

The Language of Training

WHEN A PERSON begins to train a dog for the first time, the amount of new information can be staggering. I hope to simplify certain terminology that will make comprehension of training dogs and the events that accompany this process a bit simpler.

The terms I mention here are those you might hear from many different quarters in the dog world. When you are near the completion of your training, you may become more interested in the competitive events, which are an inherent part of the training process. I will attempt to define these events and give you some idea of who can enter.

Competitive events are evaluations of a handler and his or her dog's performance as compared to a perfect performance pictured in the judge's mind. The handler and the dog are judged against a set of rules and regulations stated by the Kennel Club of the country in which the competition occurs.

GRADUATION

Dog Obedience schools usually have graduation activities for those individuals enrolled in their school. The exercises are usually patterned on the Obedience rules and regulations, but may be adapted for their own students. Occasionally, some schools will permit other individuals to enter for a nominal fee, and depending on the school's restrictions, the dog may or may not be required to be a registered purebred. Each club or school may have its own unique restrictions.

LICENSED OBEDIENCE TRIALS

These competitions are funded primarily by people involved with purebred dogs, and the events are licensed by the Kennel Club within a respective country. The rules and regulations for these competitions are made available through the Kennel Clubs for a nominal fee. Licensed Obedience Trials are for dogs that have been registered in the records of the Kennel Club licensing the Obedience Trial, and there are specific rules as to who is eligible to enter. These competitions differ from country to country. If you are interested in competitive Obedience, you should obtain a copy of the rules and regulations from the licensing body (i.e., AKC, UKC, CKC) in your country.

SANCTIONED MATCH

Dog clubs will hold matches that are called Sanctioned Matches. These are Obedience events for dogs that meet the requirements for entry into a licensed Obedience Trial. Unlike the licensed trial, *you cannot earn credit toward a title* in a Sanctioned Match, though the rules for a Sanctioned Match are identical to those required in a licensed Obedience Trial.

CORRECTION MATCH

In these matches you can correct your dog if it does something wrong while performing. In a formal licensed Obedience Trial or a Sanctioned Match, you cannot administer a correction in the ring. The Correction Match, however, permits you the opportunity to correct your dog *in the ring*. Correction Matches are patterned on the Obedience Trial, with the aforementioned exception.

THE OBEDIENCE FUN MATCH

The fun match *loosely* follows the rules of the licensed Obedience Trial and may contain other exercises that are simply fun to do. A dog is not required to be registered to compete in these competitions. Usually, the hosting dog club will advertise their events in a brochure or flyer, which informs the exhibitor of the types of classes offered, who can enter, the entry fee, the name of the judge and the date, time and location of the event. It usually includes a list of prizes, as well as other pertinent information regarding the event. These lists are usually available at any Obedience Trial or dog event.

PHENOTYPE

The traits that are both physically and psychologically obvious to anyone observing the dog are said to be phenotypical.

If a three-legged bitch and a three-legged male were bred together and they produced four-legged puppies, the parents would be considered phenotypically three-legged and genotypically four-legged. In other words, what you actually can see in the parents is the phenotype. The genotype is what they produce when bred, and these traits very often cannot be as obviously visible as the example quoted above.

This class is lining up for the Long Sit at a Sanctioned Match.

This Lakeland Terrier is practicing the Utility *Bar Jump* at an Obedience Fun Match. Note that the *Bar Jump* is not set at full height, the jumps are not regulation distance from each other and the handler is giving an exaggerated signal.

METHODS: COMPULSION VS. REINFORCEMENT

There are only two actual motivational and conditioning methods in training, and they are diametrically opposed. "Compulsion" is the use of physical or psychological force that employs pressure and/or pain, and fear. Compulsion in simple terms is "making the dog do it." "Reinforcement" of behavior is accomplished through punishment, i.e., negative reinforcers, or through praise and reward, which are positive reinforcers.

"Inducement" is to lead or draw the dog into responding in the desired manner. Inducive methods afford the dog at least two choices and require decision on the dog's part. Reinforcement of desired behavior patterns is accomplished with positive reinforcers when a desired response is obtained, and the absence of any reinforcers when an incorrect response is performed. The normal procedure is to utilize "successive approximation" (a form of operant conditioning) to "grow" the desired behavior response.

REINFORCER

A stimulus that follows a response is a reinforcer. It is the result of a particular action and normally causes the activity to be repeated.

POSITIVE REINFORCER

A reward that produces a satisfying state of affairs in the animal is a positive reinforcer. An example of a physical positive reinforcer would be a pat administered after the dog has exhibited a desirable action. A psychological positive reinforcer would be the use of the term "good."

REWARD

The administration of something *after* the animal has responded in some manner is a reward. Usually this is positive reinforcement.

PUNISHMENT

A reaction that produces an unwanted state of affairs in the animal is punishment. A physical example of this would be a slap under the chin for an action that you don't want repeated. A psychological example would be a scolding.

NEGATIVE REINFORCER

A reward that removes an unwanted state of affairs in the animal is referred to as a negative reinforcer. A physical example of the negative reinforcer would be the pressure administered on your dog's rump to make it sit. This pressure is uncomfortable and is removed once your dog is sitting. The actual removal of this pressure from the dog's hindquarters is a physical example of negative reinforcement. If you were to scold your dog for doing something, and then stop the scolding when a desired action began to happen, you would be employing the negative reinforcer in a psychological manner.

PRIMARY REINFORCER

A primary reinforcer is anything that satisfies a biological need in the animal. Some examples of primary reinforcers and the biological needs they fulfill are:

Primary reinforcer	Biological need satisfied (Drive)
(1) Food	Feeding drive
(2) Sex	Pairing drive
(3) Car chasing	Protective drive
(4) Fear of a person	Protective drive

PRIMITIVE DRIVES

A species possesses certain instinctive, primitive drives in order to survive and provide a continuation of the species. There are three main primitive drives:

(1) The protective drive
(2) The pairing drive (sex drive)
(3) The feeding drive

The protective drive exists in one of two states: fight or flight. This drive cannot exist in both states simultaneously. It is all-consuming to the animal and it completely subjugates all other drives and moods. In other words, once engaged you cannot appeal to another mood or drive. The dog that is fearful cannot be appealed to with food, and when in a fight, the last thing that crosses a dog's mind is sex or food.

SECONDARY REINFORCEMENT

Secondary reinforcements are stimuli that are paired with a reduction of drive stimuli. This means that when your dog performs a command well, you give praise followed by a treat. In short order the dog will think of the praise as being as good as receiving the treat. The praise is the secondary reinforcement, while the food (treat) is the primary reinforcer. As time goes on in the training process, you want to rely more and more on the secondary reinforcement—praise. As the dog receives more and more food during training, the feeding drive is reduced. This is why the secondary reinforcer should be given *before* the primary reinforcer is administered.

AGGRESSIVENESS

It never ceases to amaze me how this term is misused within the dog world. Many people automatically think of the "biting" dog as an example of this term. This, in fact, is not the case.

Aggressiveness is a quality of temperament that you want in a dog when it comes to training—in other words, *it is a desirable trait.*

I read advertisements in the local newspapers all the time

under the "help wanted" column. A young, aggressive man or woman is wanted. The last thing an employer wants is a person who will run out and bite prospective clients or customers. Aggressiveness is the same in terms of human and canine temperament. *Aggressiveness means that the animal is capable of presenting a positive response to a positive stimulus.* For example, a dog that pursues a thrown ball is giving a positive response to a positive stimulus—the dog is demonstrating aggressiveness. A person who walks toward a dog while the dog is moving toward the person is, by definition, acting aggressively. The dog that barks or attempts to bite a person is demonstrating *hostile* aggressiveness.

Aggressiveness in any dog that is destined for a little training can be a good quality.

CLASSICAL CONDITIONING

Classical or Pavlovian conditioning occurs when an unconditioned stimulus evokes an unconditioned response (elicited response). This is what Pavlov discovered when a dog was subjected to the ringing of a bell when the animal was allowed to taste food powder. The bell came to be known as the "unconditioned stimulus," while the food powder became known as the "conditioned stimulus." Soon, because the dog associated the ringing of the bell with the food powder, the dog would salivate (a reflexive reaction) at the first sound of the bell. The result (salivation) was an unconditioned response.

OPERANT CONDITIONING

Operant conditioning can be explained most easily using the following example: You are driving a car down a deserted road at four A.M. There is no traffic anywhere to be seen, but when you see the traffic light ahead suddenly turn red, you automatically reach for the brake, even though you know there is no other traffic. This is the *result* of operant conditioning.

Reinforcers are used to guide or shape emitted behaviors in the dog, and are therefore part of the dog's operant conditioning.

CHARACTER

Character is the stability of a dog's attitude that allows the dog to ignore disruptions of any sort. For example, a dog that is using its nose to follow a track of a human being encounters another dog that has rushed up to a nearby fence barking furiously. The first dog continues to follow the track completely undisturbed, exhibiting a stable character. Even if this is the result of an animal that has been well trained, stability of character is evident in the dog's responsiveness to training.

ENVIRONMENT

Environment has little to do with the actual physical surroundings of the animal. It really has to do with how the dog perceives its surroundings. A garbage can located on the sidewalk may be something that the dog observes daily with little reaction; yet the same can when viewed by the dog at night may be perceived as something hostile.

GUN SHYNESS

True gun shyness is the negative response to a sound stimulus that contains a large number of odd harmonics. It is not the volume of the sound the dog responds to, but the odd harmonics. This is why some dogs go into a state of panic whenever they detect a thunderstorm, even if it is too far away for their owner to hear. Not only does the dog go into a panic, but noticeable motor tremors can be detected on the inside of the dog's thigh. The dog cannot control this reaction. A dog can overcome the fear of loud noises, but cannot overcome a negative response to a sound that has a great number of odd harmonics. True gun shyness is a defect in the dog's sympathetic nervous system and is something that you cannot correct to any marked degree.

INSTINCTS

Instincts are definitely "species specific." They are inherited. Some examples of instincts follow:

(1) Tracking
(2) Hunting
(3) Shaking of prey
(4) Circling to lie down
(5) Burying bones
(6) Marking territory
(7) Retrieving

During the dog's upbringing, these instincts can be enhanced or subjugated.

MOODS VS. DRIVES

Moods are a craving for activity that originate internally or externally. This craving declines with time. Some examples are:

Moods of:	Moods for:
Belonging	Hunting
Rejection	Deliberation
Playfulness	Sex

Drives are conditions that originate from within the organism, *not externally.* Drives are goal-oriented and will only subside once the goal has been achieved.

Moods are psychological traits that can be utilized as a reinforcer when teaching/training a dog. Because moods originate from outside the organism they can be intensified by the handler for use as a reinforcer. For example, the mood of "belonging" can be intensified by isolating the dog for several moments before you use this mood as a reinforcer. When you return, the isolation has intensified the mood for belonging, and the praise you administer has a greater meaning to the dog.

Drives, as mentioned, come from within the organism. The dog either has the drive or it doesn't. The effective trainer attempts to appeal to a mood when training, and hopes to engage a drive. In training, learning will result most quickly if a drive has been engaged.

MOTIVATION

Motivation provides a "motive," or a reason, for taking a certain action. Motivation comes before the fact, while reinforcement comes after the fact.

CONFIDENCE

Confidence is a dog's self-assuredness. It is obtained from being in one's own territory, being the pack leader or reliance on itself. It may come from any one of these things or a combination of them. A dog usually exhibits the greatest amount of confidence when on its own property, and the farther away from it, the lower the confidence. A German Shepherd Dog may aggressively pursue a small Dachshund along the street, but the closer the small dog gets to its own property, the greater its confidence becomes, so that when the little dog arrives at home, the roles may reverse. The small dog turns around and begins to pursue the German Shepherd Dog in an obviously hostile aggressive manner. The German Shepherd Dog then runs back toward *its* own property, where the rules once again reverse.

The same confidence increases in the presence of a dog's owner, who usually serves as the dog's pack leader.

SOVEREIGNTY

Sovereignty is the attitude presented showing that a dog is "king" of wherever it happens to be. It signifies the utmost in confidence, and the dog takes this attitude wherever it goes, regardless of the territory or the proximity of the pack leader.

This attitude is an inner feeling of rank, power and authority. It is displayed in everything the dog does. Another common term for this attitude of self-assuredness that is commonly used among dog people is "presence." This is a valuable asset in both Conformation and Obedience competition.

SUCCESSIVE APPROXIMATION (SHAPING)

A complex maneuver can be broken into easily reinforced steps that become progressively more demanding. The result is a behavior "shaped" toward the desired response. This process is called successive approximation and is the main feature of operant conditioning.

THRESHOLD OF SENSATION

This is the specific point level (quantitative) from which a dog begins to react to a given external stimulus—it is the amount or quantity of stimuli that finally causes a dog to react in some manner.

(1) Lower threshold = reacts to less stimulus
(2) Higher threshold = reacts to a greater degree of stimulus
(3) The ideal threshold of sensation occurs when the dog reacts to a "normal" level of stimulus.

LEARNING

By definition, learning is the acquisition of new responses or the enhanced execution of old ones. The greater the psychological impact that the reinforcer has on the dog, the greater its speed of learning.

TRAINING

Training is the repetitious practice of a conditioned response that has already been learned.

THE LAWS OF LEARNING

Psychologists have established that there are three laws that govern learning within all organisms, whether human, canine or any other species. These laws came as the result of work accomplished by Thorndike under the tutelage of B. F. Skinner:

(1) The law of readiness
(2) The law of effect
(3) The law of exercise

The law of readiness: In order for a reinforcer to have the desired effect on the dog (organism), the dog has to be prepared and must want to receive the reinforcer. Therefore, food will have no effect on a satiated dog.

The law of effect is the effect the reinforcer has on the dog (organism). A leg of roast beef administered at a high rate of speed to the top of the dog's head will not have the same effect as that of a tidbit fed to a hungry dog.

The law of exercise is simply practice, practice, practice; however, if requested to perform over and over again ritualistically, the exercise may be perceived as a punishment by the dog.

SCHEDULES OF REINFORCEMENTS

The frequency at which a reinforcer is administered for a particular performance has a direct bearing on the rate at which material is learned and retained.

For an action to be learned in the shortest time, a schedule of reinforcement should be supplied every time the correct response is given. The correct time between given positive reinforcers has to do with what is called a "fixed ratio" schedule, but let it suffice to say that every time the dog performs, reinforcement should be given.

Over a period of time the schedule of reinforcement has to be altered to a point where the dog cannot anticipate when the reinforcer will be forthcoming. This type of schedule, where the learning takes place quickly and is retained, is called a "variable ratio" of reinforcement. In this manner the dog never knows when a reinforcement will be given.

To bridge the gap between a fixed ratio and a variable ratio of reinforcement, I find that an "interval ratio" works the best—that is, the interval between reinforcers is predictable. For example, sometimes a positive reinforcer is given at an interval of every third, sixth or even tenth time that the performance is correct.

Ideally, the positive reinforcer should be administered at various times that are unknown to the dog. In other words, the dog cannot predict when the tidbit is going to be given.

ELIMINATION OF A BEHAVIOR

It never ceases to amaze me when I hear people say they honestly believe the way to stop a behavior is through punishment. Punishment, whether you like the idea or not, *is* a reinforcement (reward). If you want a behavior to be eliminated, then *ignore* it. If you don't react to it or remember it, neither will the dog. Punishment might make *you* feel good, but it will not stop the unwanted behavior; instead, it will become a learned response. The dog is obviously getting something pleasurable out of the unwanted behavior, which is attention. You have to remove the niceness from the behavior, but not by punishing. Ensure that at the moment your dog begins to do whatever it is you want to stop, something that is unpleasant is the result of the action. At the same time, ignore the actions.

TEMPERAMENT

This term is a highly qualitative characteristic that is both breed specific and function specific. Good temperament means a dog possesses all of the psychological characteristics inherent in a given breed. The type of temperament you would expect to find in a Basset Hound is not the same as you would expect in a German Shepherd Dog. This is because temperament is "breed specific." On the other hand, should the dog in question have the necessary temperament characteristics needed for a particular *task*, it is "function specific."

If a dog is required for a specific function, and if all the psychological and physical attributes required for that function are present, the dog has "good temperament." Every dog owner has a concept of how pronounced or to what degree these attributes should be present. The attributes are therefore quantitative. This means that "good" temperament is really in the eye of the beholder.

TRACTABILITY

Tractability is the most important single characteristic of temperament that any dog destined for training could have. It is a measure of a dog's willingness to respond to directions. It reflects itself in a willingness to learn, a desire to please and attentiveness.

BRAVERY VS. COURAGE

Bravery is a quality produced by certain high threshold components. Its absolute degree is called fearlessness. It is not found in normal individuals because it completely negates some responses necessary for survival. A brave dog enjoys a fight just for the sake of fighting, and no thought process is required—the dog just reacts. The opposite of bravery is shyness.

On the other hand, courage is the dog's willingness to subjugate its own personal safety in the interest of the pack or pack leader. When the pack or pack leader is threatened and the dog intervenes, and in so doing risks personal injury, courage is demonstrated. Thought processes are required. Bitches are usually higher in courage than males, while males are higher in bravery. The opposite of courage is cowardice.

A dog may have a pronounced degree of either bravery or of courage, but not the same degree of both temperament characteristics.

APPENDIX

Obedience Trainer's Checklist

In all Obedience training there must be a schedule that you will follow in order to have a trained dog. There should also be a particular order that you will follow to accomplish this feat. That is what this chapter is meant to do. A Trainer's Checklist is in fact a schedule of events organized in the order that you should follow to have an Obedience trained dog. To recap:

- Training your dog in Obedience should only take about one hour per day, but not done all at one time.
- The younger your dog, the shorter the attention span will be.
- Ensure that one person does all the training until the dog has been trained to at least the ninth lesson.
- Select a place to do your training that is devoid of distractions and one where you have the dog's undivided attention.
- Your place of residence is also your dog's place of refuge and should be kept as such. Even if you take your dog to a place just a block away from home, it will learn more quickly. Your dog feels much the same as you probably feel—that the home is not a place of work.

CHECKING YOUR PROGRESS

LESSON ONE

In General

- First, do not feed your dog until *after* a training session has been concluded. Your dog works better on an empty stomach at any rate. Second, if you are taking your dog out to train away from home, take a plastic bag for cleanup along with you.
- If you like your pet, inoculations are needed for protection and good health, especially rabies and booster shots.
- Use the technique described in chapter 2 to place the training collar on your dog.
- When your dog does something well, praise as much as is possible.
- Should your dog act up and require a scolding, follow the examples given (see chapter 2).

Heeling

- When you step off on the right foot, check the position of your dog as described in chapter 2. You will be amazed at how quickly your dog will learn to anticipate a walk when you step off on your right foot. If correctly positioned beside you, praise your dog effusively.
- You cannot administer too much praise when your dog is in the correct position.
- Should your dog attempt to balk at moving with you, use a sharp jerk and *insist* on its Heeling with you no matter what.
- For example, if a $500 bill was nailed to a fence post down the street and you had one minute to get it with your dog, would you stop to wait for your dog?

Sitting

- Every time you go to the mailbox or the corner store, make it a heeling session. Whenever you reach a curb, insist that your dog Sit.

- The more times the dog has to Sit, the quicker it will learn to Sit when you stop.
- For the large breeds of dogs, as you arrive at a point where you want to stop, command your dog to Sit and then place your left forearm behind your dog's stifles (knees). Fist closed, pull back on the leash and push gently forward with your left forearm so that it is similar to someone catching you behind the knees while you are attempting to stand up straight.

LESSON TWO

- All turns are made by pivoting on the ball of the left foot. The trick to all of the turns is in the sequence of events and how they are accomplished:

  A. Pivot
  B. Turn
  C. Command to Heel
  D. Sharp jerk in the new direction
  E. Praise

  Remember, the jerk is administered *after* the turn has been made.
- Exhibiting dogs during a graduation or an Obedience competition requires that you perform the turns in a different manner.
- As you start into a turn or a change in pace (fast–slow–normal), always phase into the change easily by altering your pace ever so slightly, which will forewarn your dog that something is about to happen.
- Almost imperceptibly slow your pace down, and within one or two paces come to a stop with your left foot at a right angle to your right foot (make a "T"). Turn about so as to bring your right foot up to your left foot at a right angle (make an "L"). Bring your left foot up alongside of your right foot so that you are standing with your two feet side by side.

Helping a large dog learn to "Sit."

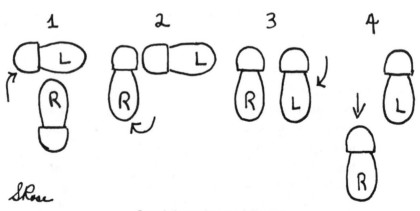

Completing a change of direction.

- STATIONARY RIGHT TURN. This exercise is started when you have your dog sitting at your left side. Make sure that the sequence of events is correct, namely:

  A. Use your dog's name to get attention and wait for what is about to happen.
  B. Give your dog the command to Heel.
  C. Simultaneously, take half a step to your right and administer a sharp jerk in this new direction parallel to the ground.

- RIGHT TURN
  LEFT TURN
  ABOUT TURN
  CIRCLE RIGHT
  Endeavor to keep your left foot on the ground as you are executing the three turns, each one a little more than 90 degrees.
- CHANGE IN PACE (fast and slow). When you change your pace from a normal pace into a slow or fast pace, ensure that you phase into the change of pace so that your speed shows a definite change without making it abrupt.
- STAYS. Begin by stepping in front of your dog, which should be Sitting as per the instructions given on pages 38–40.

LESSON THREE

- "NO." While reminding your dog to Stay, gradually take a single step back until you are at the end of the lead, standing in front of your dog and reminding it to Stay, like a broken record. While in this position, either have another person coax your dog or throw a ball, and the very moment your dog *starts* to move to break, administer the "no" (cease and desist) command but always ensure that the lead remains slack. Do not apply any sort of corporal punishment.
- While you are reminding your dog to Stay and it is remain-

Press down

Sweep out

SRone

If your dog does not respond to the hand signal for Down, return to the Heel position. Kneeling by your dog, use the right hand to sweep the dog's front legs out and your left hand to press on the dog's shoulders.

R L

R

L

SRone

The return around your dog. Walk into the Heel position while supporting the lead with your left hand.

ing in position, very quietly say "good" without so much enthusiasm as to make it break position.

- Don't create problems by attempting to correct your dog with a jerk. *A dog is never jerked on the Stay*—the jerk is administered whenever you want the dog to move, e.g., Heeling or Coming.
- LEAVE YOUR DOG and go to the END of the LEAD. Let go of all of the lead and put the loop into the left hand. Command to Stay and signal with the flat right hand. Pause. Walk directly to the end of the lead while reminding the dog to Stay.
- STEP BACK and CALL YOUR DOG. This is the first in a series of maneuvers that will make up the Recall exercise. Follow the instructions as per pages 44–45.
- THE STAND. Put the lead into the left hand and perform as per pages 45–47. The most important feature of this training maneuver is that the lead remain slack at all times. A tight lead at any time could signal to your dog to Sit.
- OBSTACLE HEELING as per pages 47–49. Allow your dog the opportunity to make a few mistakes and let it figure out how to get out of the predicament.
- THE DOWN. Give the command as the right hand is going up so that your dog will begin to understand that the raising of the hand means Down.
- When practicing the Stay, in a Sitting or Down position at the end of the lead, increase the time until your dog is Staying for three minutes. Should your dog break position, take care that you do *not* administer a jerk on the lead.

LESSON FOUR

- STAYS. Leave your dog and go to the end of the lead. Drop the lead on the ground and then stand on the end of the lead. Continue to remind the dog to Stay while standing on the end of the lead. Take one step back while increasing the time from one–two–three minutes.

- RETURN AROUND YOUR DOG. Walk at a normal speed around your dog's left side, then behind your dog and up to your dog's right side (your left side—heeling position), while supporting the lead at about the midpoint between your thumb and forefinger of your left hand, until you come up to your dog in the Heeling position.
- THE FINISH. As per the instructions on page 53.
- THE STAND. For trainers of Obedience training classes, have the students perform the Stand on their own accord on one single command, "Stand your dogs."

LESSON FIVE

- LEFT HAND off the LEAD. As per the instructions on page 63.
- CIRCLE RETURN. As per the instructions on page 64.
- DOWN from the FRONT. Step immediately in front of your dog so that its nose is immediately in front of your knees. As you raise your hand up as high as it will go, issue the command "Down." Drop to your right knee in front of your dog and use your right hand to administer a jerk downward on your lead by grasping it about two inches from the collar. Keep the singular pressure downward on your lead until your dog is down.
- FIGURE EIGHT. Be sure to include a start in both the directions. As your dog learns this exercise, the practice session should include two changes of pace and two halts.

Without any doubt, one of the last exercises is the most important Heeling exercise that you will encounter and should be practiced every day of your dog's training.

A shopping plaza is the ideal location provided that you use the section that is remote from heavy human traffic flow. In this manner your dog will see and hear the movement of the vehicles and people surrounding the mall, and will soon discover that you still insist on the same type of behavior as in other surroundings.

- THE SIT in MOTION. This means that you are about to get your dog into a Sitting position without depressing your dog's rear. If you are following the instructions given, use your peripheral vision to see if your dog is starting to come to a Sitting position.
- DIMINISH the FINISH.
- BACK UP and CALL YOUR DOG. Ensure that you are already moving backward and that you have released all the lead except the loop so that your dog will feel the jerk.
- RECALL USING FOOD.
  SELECTION of FOOD. The food you are going to use is not to feed your dog; instead it will be used as a physical, positive reinforcer during the training. First, it should be of the type of food that your dog would relish. The food you select should be people-type of food—cheese, steak leftovers or wieners. Second, it should be of a type that requires no chewing as a bone would. Something that is gone in one gulp would be the best.
- SIT and DOWN with the LEAD on the GROUND beside the dog. When you are at half the full distance (five paces) away from your dog, and then at the full distance (ten paces), increase the time to one minute and then two minutes and finally three minutes duration. If your dog breaks position from any distance, return to his side and start again. After you have scolded your dog at the moment it breaks position, it is best to start again. Reassure the dog at a close distance for a short time period and give praise for staying.

LESSON SIX
- LEAD over the SHOULDER HEELING. While the right hand still holds onto the lead, your left hand can seize the lead and anticipate using any corrective jerks if need be.
- STRAIGHTEN the SITS
- SITS in MOTION as per the instructions given on pages 74–75. but with no command or forewarning.

- STAND for EXAMINATION as per the instructions given on page 82.
- RECALLS and FOOD for SITTING. Ensure the tidbit is given for the action of sitting whether crooked or not. First you were giving your dog the treat for just coming to you, then for coming to you and Sitting when the dog arrived and finally for Sitting close and straight in front of you. Don't hesitate to go back even to stepping in front of your dog. You can only administer an effective correction when you are up close to your dog.

LESSON SEVEN

- LEAD TRAILING HEELING. Bear in mind that the lead trailing (or off lead) is a dog's privilege, not a right. Any action of your dog contrary to good heeling means that it is back on the lead immediately.
- FINISH. The food should be used as per the instructions on pages 90–93.
- RECALL and TARGET changes the moment that you administer the use of food.
- HEELING with a LIGHT LINE. At this stage of training your dog should know what a jerk on the collar means and you should be able to replace the lead with a light line, such as a piece of fishing line of about twenty-pound test. Cut a length about four feet in length and place a very small snap on one end of it so that you can connect it to the collar. Put a loop on the other end of the line or, if you have a large dog, attach a small piece of dowel that can be grasped if the need arises.

    Pretend to snap off the lead so that the dog can hear it. Make the dog think it does not have the control of the lead. The first time your dog starts to act up, administer a sharp jerk on the fishing line. You shouldn't require anywhere near as powerful a jerk at this stage of your dog's training provided you have completed the training format as described thus far.

LESSON EIGHT

Now is the time to test your dog's response to the commands. Set up a routine for you and your dog to follow that is similar to the following:

- HEELING on LEAD. Set up a pattern that includes at least two about-turns, two right-hand turns and two left-hand turns. Put into the pattern one change in pace from normal to slow and also normal to fast. Set up one figure-eight pattern that includes at least two complete figure-eight patterns and two halts.

- STAND for EXAMINATION. Have a second person stationed close by so that you can Stand your dog and they can run a hand over your dog, touching your dog's head, shoulders and back. You should not tell your dog to Stay more than once.

- HEELING off LEAD. Perform the same pattern that you just did when your dog was on lead but perform the exercise off lead.

- RECALL. Place your dog beside you and on one command to Stay, leave your dog for about fifteen paces without having to repeat the command. Turn to face your dog, and then on one single command, use your dog's name and the command to Come.

- LONG SIT. Place your dog beside you, give a single command with a signal to Stay. Pause momentarily and then walk directly away from your dog about fifteen paces. Once there, turn to face your dog and remain in that position for about one minute. Returning to your dog's side completes this exercise.

- LONG DOWN. Place your dog beside you at your left-hand side. When you are ready, issue the command and hand signal for your dog to lie down. Walk directly away from your dog about fifteen paces, and without a sound wait for three minutes before returning around your dog. At this stage of the training your dog should be a trained dog.

If your dog can perform all these exercises correctly, and should you have the inclination to enter into a graduation or an Obedience match, contact an Obedience training club in your area. Most training groups are willing to assist you. To perfect your dog's performance you should be training in all forms of distractions, with both other people and other dogs nearby.

Congratulations—you have now successfully taught your dog the exercises to complete the Novice Obedience title. Your best friend is now a true Companion Dog.

Contemplating a reward for a job well done.